Become What You Say, Second Edition:

How Your Positive Words, Thoughts, and Actions
Shape Your Accomplishments

Gabe Hamda, Ph.D., SPHR

ICATT Consulting
www.icatt.net
January 2018
Second Edition

Dear Thomas
Want to achieve
greatness?
① freely give
Love
② Make a
difference
Thank you
Gabe
12/16/2017
Twin Cities

Become What You Say 2nd Edition: How Your Positive Words, Thoughts, and Actions Shape Your Accomplishments

Printed in the United States of America

ISBN 978-0-578-19986-3

Dedication

Become What You Say, Second Edition:
How Your Positive Words, Thoughts, and Actions Shape Your Accomplishments

This book is dedicated to two worthy community service initiatives.

Go Pro21 Community is dedicated to inspiring you to achieve your highest human potential so that (a) you have a decent quality of life; (b) you are capable of contributing to your community; and (c) you are a positive force as a global citizen.

Access Growing Business Council fosters growing businesses to create good paying jobs to grow the local economy. Access Growing Business Council creates synergy for accelerated business growth that positively contributes to the local community and to society at large.

100% of sales profits from this book will be dedicated to the advancement of the mission of these two worthy community initiatives.

Table of Contents

Gratitude

I am blessed to be surrounded by loving, talented, wise, and dedicated family and friends who helped me write this book.

Many thanks to my wife Jenny and daughter Elshadai for their encouragement and for creating space for me to complete this book. More importantly, Jenny and Elshadai have provided much needed constructive and honest inputs. While this project required that I borrow significant time away from family time, Jenny and Elshadai granted me the grace and understanding with the knowledge that this book is our small but precious gift to make our world a beautiful place to live.

I am indebted to my editorial team, which consists of Shari Weaver and Jonathan Tessier, who formed an amazing team to help deliver this book with quality, clarity, and on schedule. Aside from editing the entire book, Shari provided much needed advice on content, structure, and flow. Both Shari and Jonathan created an encouraging and nurturing environment for me to be at my best. Their demonstrated composure meant so much. Jonathan provided insightful advice on messaging clarity and created the visual appeal of the book. I am grateful to the talented Allie Engley, who created the graphics and provided production advice for the 1st edition of this book.

I am also grateful for those who allowed me to use their life stories to include in the book to inspire our readers.

— Gabe Hamda, Ph.D., SPHR

Preface

In writing the second edition of this book, I have two distinct audiences: (1) those who are dedicated to making our world a better place; and (2) those who are improving living conditions for themselves and their immediate family members. While these two types of people are not mutually exclusive, we all emphasize one over the other at different stages of our lives.

This book is primarily for people who have a worthy goal to accomplish. A worthy goal is a goal beyond a person's personal interest and bigger than oneself. Some examples of worthy goals include: eliminating hunger from the face of the earth, eliminating childhood obesity in the nation, eliminating bullying in schools, providing free college educational access to needy students, and eliminating sexual harassment from the workplace. This book provides the right frame of mind to accomplish an impossible but worthy goal.

This book is primarily for those who are pursuing a goal bigger than themselves.

The book is secondarily for people who want to achieve positive quality of life outcomes. Positive quality of life outcomes include such things as good health, meaningful relationships, career success, happiness, and satisfaction with one's accomplishments.

How does the message in this book help the two groups of people?
Your thoughts are at the root of your words. Your choice to use positive words becomes positive self-talk. In practicing positive self-talk, you encourage yourself to achieve a goal, provide instructions to complete complex tasks, evaluate your actions for continuous improvement, and focus your attention to achieve excellence.

While positive thoughts and self-talk set the tone for your life's direction, the book also features positive actions that enrich your life. These actions include reflective planning, generosity, gratitude, networking, coopetition-oriented teamwork, giving back to your community, and pursuing excellence.

If you are contemplating achieving a huge goal, improving your quality of life, and adding meaning and fulfillment to your life, this is a book you must read. The book combines serious research with practical action steps you can implement. This is a hands-on and interactive workbook that includes a self-assessment for each topic, success stories, practice questions, and discussion questions. The content is presented in question and answer format in anticipation of your own questions about each subject area. Reflective questions and applications are included to allow you to apply the skills you learn in the book.

The formula this book presents is:

Worthy Goal Achievement Formula

Accomplishment of Your Worthy Goal =

Your Positive Thoughts

Your Positive Words

Your Positive Actions

Chapter 1

Introduction: Become What You Say, Second Edition
How Your Positive Words, Thoughts, and Actions
Shape Your Accomplishments

Book Selected Quotes

❝ ❞

The tongue has the power of life and death, and those who love it will eat its fruit.
— Proverbs 18:21

You have been criticising yourself for years and it has not worked. Try approving of yourself and see what happens.
— Louise Hay

A goal without a plan is just a wish.
— Antoine de Saint-Exupéry

We make a living by what we get. We make a life by what we give.
— Winston Churchill

It's not happiness that brings us gratitude; it's gratitude that brings us happiness.
— Unknown.

The successful networkers I know, the ones receiving tons of referrals and feeling truly happy about themselves, continually put the other person's needs ahead of their own.
— Bob Burg

Talent wins games, but teamwork and intelligence wins championships.
— Michael Jordan

A flower does not think of competing to the flower next to it. It just blooms.
— Zen Chin

Only a life lived for others is a life worthwhile.
— *Albert Einstein*

Book Abstract

Positive Self-Talk: Positive self-talk means using words that are self-fulfilling, self-affirming, and self-encouragement in your communications. Positive self-talk produces optimistic outcomes in your immediate actions as well as your long-term life. Why? Research shows that positive self-talk provides positive energy, determination, and persistent effort that yields outcomes you wish to achieve.

Reflective Planning: The beginning of a new season is a good time for planning what to accomplish in the time ahead. A new season can be a new year, a birthday, an anniversary, or a life changing situation. Reflective planning is a friendly tool for gently reflecting on your past successes and your values in order to map out a successful future.

Generosity: Acts of generosity make our world a better place. If we all only look out for ourselves and our own kind, our world will be a miserable place. Giving time and being emotionally generous can be as valuable as giving money. Acts of generosity make a difference in the lives of recipients whether the recipients are individuals or organizations or communities. There is extensive research that demonstrates the benefits of generosity to the giver. For example, one of the notable researchers on generosity, Dr. Stephen Post, writes: "The remarkable bottom line of the science of love is that giving protects overall health twice as much as aspirin protects against heart disease." Post reports that giving to others has been shown to increase health benefits in people with chronic illness including HIV, multiple sclerosis, and heart problems.

Gratitude: Gratitude is a feeling of appreciation or thanks for what an individual receives that may be tangible or intangible. Research shows that people who practice gratitude reap the benefits of improved physical health, feeling more positive emotions, relishing good experiences, dealing with adversity, building strong relationships increased energy, optimism, and empathy. Regardless of how well you rate yourself in practicing gratefulness now, practice will increase your gratitude and expressing it will become more natural. As you become a more grateful person, your return on investment will keep increasing.

Networking: Networking is making friends at your every interaction with others. Networking is strengthening your existing relationships and making new positive relationships. Networking is the most powerful interpersonal skills you may use to accomplish your personal interest goals as well as your community interest goals. The more you learn and practice networking, the more effective you become and the more it works for you.

Coopetition-Oriented Teamwork: Coopetition-oriented teamwork is collaboration among competing and convergent groups of people in order to achieve a common interest, mutual benefits, or higher purpose. Members of the team may be competitors, rivals, or may have divergent beliefs, backgrounds, ethnicity, skills, interests, politics, nationality, personalities, values and any combination of attributes. Coopetition-oriented teamwork is a force multiplier that can take individual efforts to new heights of accomplishment. With constant alignment of team members with the common interest and with cultivated synergies among team members, the journey and the destination of coopetition-oriented teams can be extraordinary.

Giving Back: Giving back is engaging in activities that make a difference for others. Stages of giving back include: (1) discovering your purpose; (2) volunteering; and (3) community advocacy. While giving back makes the community we live in a better place for generations to come, research studies also confirm numerous benefits for the person who gives back. Some of the benefits include: increased total health, longer life, increased happiness, and greater life fulfillment. Yes, giving back makes a real difference for others as well as for yourself.

Excellence Over Perfection: "Perfection is the enemy of good" seems counterintuitive but refers to the fact that often people freeze when trying to accomplish important tasks due to not having perfect circumstances. Ecclesiastes 11: 4 instructs "If you wait for perfect conditions, you will not get anything done." Based on extensive research findings, this chapter advocates that "you may benefit from the pursuit of excellence rather than the pursuit of perfection." While perfectionism is likely to jeopardize the wellbeing of individual contributors, teams, and organizations, the pursuit of excellence is likely to benefit all involved.

Rate Your Current Practice of *Become What You Say* Actions

Rate your current practice of *Become What You Say* actions on a scale of 1 to 5.
(1=Poor, 2=Below Average, 3=Average, 4=Good, 5=Excellent)

Become What You Say Actions	1=Poor 5=Excellent
1. When you encounter challenging situations, you tend to reframe the situation to express yourself in appreciative terms.	1 2 3 4 5
2. You frequently reflect on your successes in life to plan your future pursuits.	1 2 3 4 5
3. You believe that what and when you give makes a difference.	1 2 3 4 5
4. You readily express gratitude to people you meet in person and virtually, including online communications, emails, texts, and phone conversations.	1 2 3 4 5
5. In networking conversations, you make personal connections by trying to learn more about the person than simply what they do.	1 2 3 4 5
6. You are good at finding a common ground with your rivals.	1 2 3 4 5
7. You volunteer in at least one cause that benefits others.	1 2 3 4 5
8. You maintain positive and constructive communication with your frenemies.	1 2 3 4 5
9. You see mistakes as opportunities for growth and learning	1 2 3 4 5
10. You celebrate small achievements	1 2 3 4 5

Your total score is _____

Assess your score:

40 +	Outstanding
30 +	Very Good
25 +	Good
Below 25	Needs Improvement

"Become What You Say" Success story

Note: The purpose of this story is to illustrate the application of principles and skills covered in this book. The story is based on character elements of real people I know personally, but the details and events are my creative work designed for illustrative purposes.

Hanna is a model citizen. After reading *Become What you Say*, she challenged herself to practice all the skills and make them second nature within a year's time. She spent an entire month practicing positive self talk. She built her positive self talk in three steps: (1) kept a tally of her negative self talk and rewrote a positive self talk alternative; (2) kept a tally of her family members' negative self talk and rewrote a positive self-talk alternative; and (3) consciously used positive self talk. To ensure she stayed on track, she asked her friends to call out when she correctly used positive self talk and when she violated her pledge.

Hanna practiced the pursuit of excellence by scripting out how to accomplish her top one priority assignment. Then, she incrementally increased the number of assignments to script out and complete them minus perfectionist tendencies.

She incorporated reflective planning by completing the reflective planning spreadsheet during her August birthday and with the help of her best friend. She also talked her friend into completing the spreadsheet and working together as accountability partners on their important goals.

Hanna applied generosity by increasingly meeting the needs of the people around her with emotional and material support. At the same time, she gradually decreased her material possessions.

She started her gratitude journey by writing and sending one thank you email per day and one handwritten thank you note per month.

Hanna implemented increasing her networking skills by developing a networking checklist she followed every week. She self-rated herself on a daily basis.

She joined the local toastmasters as one of the volunteer organizers. She also decided to practice coalition building and giving back to the community. In this role, she dedicated time to help inner city youth build their professional presentation skills. At the same time, she collaborated with other like minded people to accomplish a goal.

Throughout this self-transformation process, Hanna used a dual approach of self assessment in her personal journal as well as working with a peer coach to stay on track.

Success Story Discussion Questions

1. *Which of the skills did Hanna master the most? Why?*

2. *What additional method do you suggest for Hanna to consider?*

Introduction

A growing body of knowledge and research confirms that the words and thoughts you use to address yourself play a major role in your success. Positive words build up and negative words destroy. I have been a fan and practitioner of positive self-talk for many years, and this book is dedicated to telling you about it.

This book is my gift of love to you, the reader. Thank you for buying it. Thank you for deciding to read it. I hope you enjoy it. I hope you practice it. I chose the subject, *become what you say*, as a reminder to you because by adopting positive self-talk you set yourself up for success with your very own words. How cool is that?

Background: What about your words?

Technically speaking, *words* are elements of language that carry meaning and make up sentences. More informally, *words* can mean the messages we deliver. Thus, in this book, I am going to equate *words* with the message you intend to convey.

Typically, we think of the spoken or written word as directed to others. But the majority of your words are spoken to yourself as your thoughts. This is known as *self-talk*.

I have written this book to make you aware that the words you speak to yourself have real consequences. Positive self-talk is life-giving while negative self-talk saps life.

Activity Questions

In your conversations with yourself:

- *Do you tend to make kind remarks about yourself? Yes/No*

- *Do you tend to be self-critical? Yes/No*

- *Do you tend to appreciate your life experiences? Yes/No*

- *Give examples of remarks you tell yourself?*

What is the central message of this book?

Every word that comes out of your mouth is a seed that produces a harvest of the same seed. Positive words about yourself advance your success; while negative words about yourself sabotage your cause. Therefore, be intentional with the words you use.

What are potential alternative titles of the book?

The following titles were seriously considered for this book:

- *Positivity*
- *Positively Speaking*
- *Soft Power*
- *24X7 Think Act Positive*
- *Speak Positive*
- *Managing Your Internal Self-Talk*
- *Watch What You Say About Yourself: It will Become Reality*
- *Your Words Will Seal Your Future*
- *Your Words Will Guarantee Your Level of Success*
- *Your Words are the Best Predictor of Your Future*

What qualifies me to write this book?

I have three sets of qualifications for writing this book. The first is that I am a self-declared and life-long practitioner of positive self-talk and an eternal optimist. Second, I am an expert in learning and human performance. Third, I am a storyteller and I know too many relevant stories. Below I describe my qualifications in each area.

My qualification #1 to write this book: Practitioner of positive self-talk and eternal optimist

I demonstrate my optimism through my actions, attitude, decisions, and words.

Optimism by Action:

- When I am asked to assist, I try to get it done as requested.

- When I see a need or a problem I can solve, I readily start working on a solution.

Optimism by Attitude:

- When I meet new people, I assume good intent until I see evidence otherwise.

- When I am offered constructive feedback, I accept it with gratitude rather than being defensive.

Optimism by Decisions:

- When I am offered solutions I have been looking for at the right price, I make an immediate buying decision.

- I tend to make consultant hiring decision on the spot after one networking meeting.

Optimism by Word:

- When I am asked to collaborate, I am inclined to respond: "Let's do it!" "Let's get it done." "Why not?"

- When I see people taking personal improvement actions, I tend to encourage and compliment rather than point out what they could have done differently.

I know a thing or two about optimism leading to success because I have been blessed with much success. And I enjoy every day of my life because I encounter life events as blessings.

Too often, in casual group conversations, I hear the following:

- Complaints about the boss;

- Complaints about the economy;

- Complaints about a sports team;

- Complaints about the weather;

- Complaints about the government;

- Complaints about anything someone has no control over;

- You get the idea – the list of complaints goes on and on.

What are your common topics of complaint regarding items you have no control over?

_____

_____

I do not take part in these types of "downer" conversations. Whenever complaints start, I do one or more of the following:

- Sometimes, I try to change the subject.

- I ask the participants to share an alternative viewpoint. For example, if I hear complaints about urban living, I may suggest brainstorming the advantages of urban life. You get the idea?

- When the situation permits, I point out that complaining about circumstances does not make our situation any better.

- I also may point out that repeating an event and associated emotions over and over makes us feel worse.

- I ask to share the joyous moment of the day.

- I ask to share an elevator speech.

My qualification #2 to write this book: Expert in lifelong learning and human performance

Armed with a Ph.D. in Instructional System Design and a graduate certificate in Human Resource Development, I am a practicing expert in learning and human performance development. Consequently, I have spent years exploring and studying self-directed human actions that contribute to learning and performance improvement. As a practitioner and fan of positive self-talk and optimism, I have studied best practices and research findings related to positive self-talk and human performance, including the growing body of scientific research showing a strong link between positive self-talk and improved performance. Thus, I am

17

uniquely qualified to write this book because of my personal experience with positive self-talk, positive outlook, professional and business expertise, and familiarity with scientific research on the subject.

My qualification #3 to write this book: Storyteller

I am a natural storyteller. I have been a storyteller for my entire life. Ironically, I did not know this inner talent until very recently. For every chapter in this book, I have included stories to support every hypothesis and illustrate them for greater understanding. You will be happy to read some of the most colorful and true stories. Many more will be shared during book release events.

Thus, I am qualified to write this book as (1) a master practitioner of positivity; (2) as a learning expert; and (3) as a storyteller.

What are my sources for the content of this book?

The content of this book is based on a combination of the following sources:

- Research findings on positive self-talk and related topics;

- My personal, career, and business experiences;

- Knowledge and insights based on many years of interest, study, and observation of life around me;

- Conversations with people in my networking circles; and

- Insights from listening to and reading the works of other wise people.

Who is this book written for?

In writing the second edition of this book, I have two distinct audiences (1) those who are dedicated to making our world a better place, and (2) those who are improving living conditions for themselves and their immediate family members. While these two types of people are not mutually exclusive, we all emphasize one over the other at different stages of our lives.

This book is primarily for people who have a worthy goal to accomplish. A worthy goal is a goal beyond a person's personal interest and bigger than oneself. Some examples of worthy goals include: eliminating hunger from the face of the earth, eliminating childhood obesity in the nation, eliminating bullying in schools, providing free college educational access to needy students, and eliminating sexual harassment from the workplace. This book provides the right frame of mind to accomplish an impossible but worthy goal.

The book is secondarily for people who want to achieve positive quality of life outcomes. Positive quality of life outcomes include such things as good health, meaningful relationships, career success, happiness, and satisfaction with one's accomplishments.

Who else can benefit the most from the book?

- Parents who want to use these principles to model for and teach their children;

- Career professionals who seek job satisfaction and upward mobility;

- Business owners who want to grow their businesses and create jobs in their communities;

- Political leaders, whose campaign words really matter to their electorate;

- Community leaders who are in the business of creating and spreading the common good.

How should you read this book?

I encourage you to read this book with a pen or pencil on hand to write your responses to the questions interspersed throughout. As an expert on human learning, I know that you will gain more from this book if you combine your reading with practice activities and reflective thinking. Thus, for the best results, I encourage you to make the time to actively respond to the activity questions provided throughout this book and at the end of each chapter.

What is contained in this book?

This book discusses the positive actions and benefits of:

- Positive Self-Talk: How to Reframe Your Words for Positive Action

- Reflective Planning: How Best to Mine Your Past to Guarantee Future Success

- Generosity: How Your Giving Makes a Difference

- Gratitude: How Expressing Gratitude Reaps You Abundant Joy & Happiness

- Networking: How Making Connections Generates Limitless Possibilities

- Coopetition-Oriented Teamwork: How Collaborating With Your Rivals Creates a Win-Win

- Giving Back: How One Person Has the Potential to Build a Better World

- Excellence Over Perfection: How Perfection is the Enemy of Good

How is this book different from other books?

- It is designed as a workbook with space for you to write comments and answers to activity questions. Each chapter contains at least one reflective question. You are encouraged to write your responses to the questions and act on the action items in this book.

- Each chapter contains a self-assessment to allow you to determine the level of skills you possess.

- It is written in question and answer format so you can focus on the questions that most interest you. This allows you to use your reading time wisely.

- It is designed as an interactive tool. Write on it. Underline items. You may write remarks such as agree, disagree, not sure, like it, do not like this, etc. You may draw on pages, fold them, or tear off a page and give it away. The book is written for you to do something with it.

- After you are finished with the book, you may intentionally leave it at a café for others to pick up and read.

- Important points are said over and over a little differently. Why? Habits are formed through repetition. Learning is gained through intentional repetition. Thus, the book repeats some points for reinforcement.

Success Criteria

I have set out five success criteria for this book. I will consider this book a success if the following criteria are met, in the priority order listed:

1) My number one success criterion for this book is that you, the reader, apply what you have learned here to change your life, and your enhanced positive self-talk, reflective planning, generosity, gratitude, networking skills,

coopetition-oriented teamwork, giving back to the community, and excellence over perfection.

2) My second success criterion is that you, the reader, read this book the way it is intended, taking notes, responding to the activities, and interacting with the book.

3) My third success criterion is that you, the reader, read this book however you want to read it.

4) My fourth success criterion is that you, the reader, buy the book for yourself or as a gift for someone else or receive it as a gift.

5) Finally, my fifth success criterion is that you, the reader, create your own success stories related to the ones in this book.

Thank you for considering the above five things.

If you wait for perfect conditions, you will not get anything done.
— Ecclesiastes 11: 4

Chapter 2

Positive Self-Talk
How to Reframe Your Words for Positive Action

Selected Quotes

You have been criticising yourself for years and it has not worked. Try approving of yourself and see what happens.

— Louise Hay

There are only two ways to live your life. One is as though nothing is a miracle. The other is as though everything is a miracle.

— Albert Einstein

Be careful how you think; your life is shaped by your thoughts.

— Proverbs 4:23

If you celebrate your differentness, the world will, too. It believes exactly what you tell it—through the words you use to describe yourself, the actions you take to care for yourself, and the choices you make to express yourself. Tell the world you are one-of-a-kind creation who came here to experience wonder and spread joy. Expect to be accommodated.
— Victoria Moran, *Lit From Within: Tending Your Soul For Lifelong Beauty*

But more important than the food I put into my body are thoughts I put into my mind. Thoughts of bitterness like, "I hate her!" Thoughts of despair like, "I'll never be happy again." Thoughts of fear like, "I could never do that!" And thoughts of worry, thoughts of greed and thoughts of self-loathing…"I'm so stupid." A constant diet of these killer thoughts will destroy any of us long before heartburn or cholesterol.

— Steve Goodier

You are loved, and you are worthy! Remember your wholeness. Within you is the spark of the Divine. Let go of negative self-talk and let LOVE heal you.
— Angie Karan Krezos

Abstract

Positive self-talk means using words that are self-fulfilling, self-affirming, and self-encouraging in your communications. Positive self-talk produces optimistic outcomes in your immediate actions as well as your long-term life. Why? What is the link between positive self-talk and optimistic outcomes? Research shows that positive self-talk provides positive energy, determination, and persistent effort that yields outcomes you wish to achieve.

This chapter presents positive self-talk by answering the following key questions:

- What is self-talk?

- What are the scientific theories behind positive self-talk?

- What is the empirical research evidence in support of positive self-talk?

- What are the benefits of self-talk?

- How do you develop the habit of talking positively?

- How do you reframe your negative self-talk into positive self-talk?

- Better yet, how do you develop positive self-talk as your second nature?

Positive self-talk can be learned and developed through a process of reframing. Reframing is turning negative self-talk into positive self-talk. Here is one example:

> **Negative self-talk**: *I want to learn to speak Tagalog for my upcoming project in the Philippines next year. My goodness. Tagalog is too complicated. I am not going to master it in my lifetime.*

> **Positive self-talk**: *I am going to learn Tagalog step by step. I will sign up for a Tagalog language class and hire a Tagalog language tutor. I am going to master the language by the time I travel to the Philippines to start my project.*

Given its physical, emotional, and professional benefits, positive self-talk is easy to sell. However, becoming aware of your self-talk habits, cleansing yourself of negative self-talk, and transforming to habitual positive self-talk is a long journey. With patience, time, commitment, and the application of the strategies, techniques, and tips provided in this book, you will become a full-fledged positive self-talker — a new, happier, and fulfilled self.

Rate Your Current Level of Positive Self-Talk
(1=Poor, 2=Below Average, 3=Average, 4=Good, 5=Excellent)

Positive Self Talk Actions	1=Poor 5=Excellent (Circle One)
1. You always think before you speak, even jokingly.	1 2 3 4 5
2. You know the difference between negative self-talk and positive self-talk.	1 2 3 4 5
3. When in doubt about saying something, you make positive statements about yourself and others.	1 2 3 4 5
4. When you encounter challenging situations, you reframe the situation to express yourself in appreciative terms.	1 2 3 4 5
5. You know the roles in which you naturally excel.	1 2 3 4 5
6. You invest more time in the areas where you have the most potential for greatness.	1 2 3 4 5
7. You are quick to get over a setback and try again.	1 2 3 4 5
8. You resist distractions that prevent you from achieving your goals.	1 2 3 4 5
9. You are open to learning from your experiences and from those around you.	1 2 3 4 5
10. You seize the opportunity to do what you do best, every day.	1 2 3 4 5

Your total score is _____

Assess your score:

40 +	Outstanding
30 +	Very Good
25 +	Good
Below 25	Needs Improvement

Positive Self-Talk Success Story

Note: The purpose of this story is to illustrate the application of principles and skills covered in this chapter. The story is based on character elements of real people I know personally, but the details and events are my creative work designed for illustrative purposes.

At a recent Access Growing Business Council monthly meeting, Teddy of Motivational Today presented a Positive Self-Talk and Customer Experience workshop. Participants in Teddy's workshop and members of Access Growing Business Council were: Houri, Muller, Yetti, Alamelu, Almaz, Sintayehu, DJ, Versi, Fekadu, Bernadine, Robsan, Haile, and Anita.

Here is an overview of each of the attendees, their claim to fame, and a positive self-talk remark each one made during a debriefing session of Teddy's workshop:

Houri - Co-Chair of Access and owner of her human performance consulting practice, known for super customer friendly service. Positive self-talk remark: "We are going to realize 10% growth each year by winning over one customer at a time."

Muller - Professor of finance and owner of real estate agency, known for providing customized insightful advice to real estate investors. Positive self-talk remark: "We are very good at identifying special needs of our prospects and adjusting our services to special circumstances."

Yetti - Owner of family financial empowerment enterprise, known for conducting innovative family financial management workshops that engage all members of a family regardless of age differences. Positive self-talk: "We transform members of each family into financial wizards."

Alamelu - Principal of a human capital practice, known for coaching and building resilience. Positive self-talk: "We are declaring a winning campaign for a stress-free work-life."

Almaz - Real Estate Agent, known for empowering each first time home buyer to successfully access resources to become a homeowner within 3 months of starting the process. Positive self-talk: "We believe in each first time home buyer's ability to succeed and we make it happen."

Sintayehu - Owner of Medical Services Your Way, known for providing totally individualized medical services. Positive self-talk: We totally care about your health experience and attend to your every need."

DJ - Real Estate Agent, known for accommodating a home buyer who is ready to purchase a home on day one as well as the one that requires 5 years of due diligence. Positive self-talk: "We joyfully dance to the tune of your sense of timing."

Versi - Owns her travel agency, known for anticipating and addressing direct and indirect travel related matters. Positive self-talk: "We totally eliminate stress out of your travel experience."

Fekadu - Owns software engineering company, known for speaking the language of business outcomes with technology as enabler. Positive self-talk: "We are totally fluent in your language of business."

Bernadine - Owns real estate financing brokerage, known for accurate and speedy matching of financing source with a need for investment. Positive self-talk: "If you have a viable project vision, we make sure money is a non-issue."

Robsan - Owner of a global translation interpretation company, known for instant access to language resources for every language in the world. Positive self-talk: "We are fluent in every human language."

Haile - Owner of iron work and construction management company, known for accurate and equitable pricing that guarantees cost containment and predictability for the client. Positive self-talk: "We excel in the precision of the cost of your next iron and construction work to contain your cost and give you peace of mind."

Anita - President of nonprofit technical assistance practice, best know as trusted advisor to mission oriented organizations. Positive self-talk: "We usher in effectiveness to nonprofits so that they can focus on their main mission."

Success Story Discussion Questions

What are your top three favorite businesses? Explain.

Using examples given above, write your own brief business narrative including:

Name of business:

Nature of business:

Your claim to fame:

Your positive self-talk:

What is self-talk?

Self-talk is your internal thinking which guides your outward actions. In other words, it is your internal conversation, which gets very active and very loud when you are not talking to other people. Self-talk and thinking can be used interchangeably.

Self-talk has been the subject of extensive human performance research and analysis. According to Zourbanos and associates, self-talk is one of the most commonly used mental techniques for performance enhancement. In research literature, self-talk is referred to by different yet synonymous terms such as:

- internal dialogue
- self-statements

- inner speech
- private self-talk
- self-directed speech

Positive self-talk, or positive thinking, is an optimistic version of your internal self-talk, which is constructive and encourages positive actions. Positive self-talk is an expression of self-confidence and self-worth.

Negative self-talk, or negative thinking, is a pessimistic version of your internal self-talk, which is destructive and discourages positive actions. Negative self-talk is an expression of self-doubt and second guessing your actions.

How much and how often do we talk to ourselves?

We talk to ourselves all the time. As we listen to someone speaking, our mind is also talking to us. Research indicates that most people speak at a rate of 150 to 200 words per minute, but the mind can listen to about 500 to 600 words a minute. Our internal dialogue or self-talk proceeds at a rate of 1,300 words per minute! How? Because our mind sees in pictures, and you can see a thought in a nanosecond.

Can we Push Back on the Vicious Circle of Negative Bias?

In an October 2017 article on *Forbes* online titled, *Nix The Negativity: Building Your Confidence Muscle Through Positive Self-Talk*, Deborah Goldstein explains that during episodes of negativity, our sympathetic nervous system snaps into action and releases cortisol into the bloodstream. This is the hormone responsible for our primitive impulse to "fight, flight or freeze."

Aside from its detrimental long-term health effects, cortisol fogs our minds, literally preventing us from thinking clearly. This prompts us to second-guess ourselves, leading to poor confidence and feelings of defeat, thereby looping us around once again to negative thoughts. The goal of staying positive is made more complicated by this negative feedback loop.

Goldstein further explains that evolution has equipped humans with a negativity bias. Our prehistoric ancestors had to be vigilant in every situation or risk becoming dinner for a saber-toothed tiger. This programmed our modern brains to be extra sensitive to perceived threats, even when no threat exists.

Once we have become accustomed to this level of self-imposed negativity, it takes some serious mental energy to pull ourselves back toward reality. My advice? Stay conscious of your inner voice, monitor the negativity and push back the moment you detect self-bullying.

What are the scientific theories behind positive self-talk?

A scientific theory is an explanation or model that covers a substantial group of occurrences in nature and has been confirmed by a careful examination of facts, experiments, and observations. Scientific theories that contribute to positive self-talk are: self-efficacy, learned optimism, appreciative inquiry, strength finders, and design thinking.

- **Self-efficacy** – According to psychologist Albert Bandura, self-efficacy is defined as one's belief in one's ability to succeed in specific situations or to accomplish a task.

- **Learned Optimism** – According to Martin Seligman, learned optimism is the idea in positive psychology that a talent for joy, like any other, can be cultivated. It is contrasted with learned helplessness. We learn optimism by consciously challenging negative self-talk.

- **Appreciative Inquiry** – According to David Cooperrider, appreciative inquiry gets everyone to focus on what's possible through interactive discovery and design sessions.

- **StrengthsFinders** – The Clifton StrengthsFinder measures the presence of 34 talent themes or strengths. (Talents are people's naturally recurring patterns of thought, feeling, or behavior that can be productively applied.) The more dominant a talent theme is in a person, the greater the theme's impact on that person's behavior and performance.

- **Design Thinking** – According to Bernard Roth, design thinking is a methodology used by designers to solve complex problems and find desirable solutions for clients. Design Thinking draws upon logic, imagination, intuition, and systemic reasoning, to explore possibilities of what could be, and to create desired outcomes that benefit the end user (the customer).

Matching Activity: Scientific Theories

Instructions: Match names of theories in Column B with their definitions in Column A.

Column A - Definitions of Theories	Column B- Names of Theories
___1. Focus on what's possible through interactive discovery and design sessions.	A. Design Thinking
___2. A talent for joy can be cultivated.	B. StrengthsFinders
___3. Methodology to solve complex problems and find desirable solutions.	C. Self-Efficacy
___4. Measures the presence of 34 talent themes.	D. Learned Optimism
___5. One's belief in one's ability to accomplish a task.	E. Appreciative Inquiry

Self-Efficacy Theory

Albert Bandura of Stanford University developed the theory of self-efficacy. Self-efficacy is simply a person's belief in his or her own ability. Bandura found that people who believed they could overcome their phobias were more likely to do so. The concept of self-efficacy has played a key role in educational psychology. For example, students who believe they can master a concept are more likely to do so.

In his book, *Self-Efficacy: The Exercise of Control*, Bandura demonstrates the result of over 20 years of research while comprehensively explaining the self-efficacy theory that believing one can achieve what one sets out to do results in a healthier, more effective, and generally more successful life.

Bandura and Jourden further defined self-efficacy as "people's judgements of their capabilities to organize and to execute courses of action required to attain designated types of performances." According to the self-efficacy theory, what individuals believe about their capabilities influences their motivation and as a result determines the effort and persistence in their future actions. For example, individuals with high self-efficacy have been found to exert more effort and be more persistent when faced with failure, compared to individuals with low self-efficacy. Sports psychology literature reveals a positive relationship between self-efficacy and performance in various sports such as distance running, swimming, and volleyball.

A strong sense of efficacy enhances human accomplishment and personal well-being in many ways. People with high assurance in their capabilities approach difficult tasks as challenges to be mastered rather than as threats to be avoided. Such an efficacious outlook fosters intrinsic interest and deep engrossment in activities. Furthermore, people with high self-efficacy set themselves challenging goals and maintain strong commitment to them. They heighten and sustain their efforts in the face of failure and quickly recover their sense of efficacy after failures or setbacks. They also attribute failure to insufficient effort or deficient knowledge and skills which are acquirable. They approach threatening situations with assurance that they can exercise control over them. Such an efficacious outlook produces personal accomplishments, reduces stress, and lowers vulnerability to depression.

In contrast, people who doubt their capabilities shy away from difficult tasks which they view as personal threats. They have low aspirations and weak commitment to the goals they choose to pursue. When faced with difficult tasks, they dwell on their personal deficiencies, on the obstacles they will encounter, and all kinds of adverse outcomes rather than concentrate on how to perform successfully. They also slacken their efforts and give up quickly in the face of difficulties. They are slow to recover their sense of efficacy following failure or setbacks, and, because they view insufficient performance as deficient aptitude, it does not require much failure for them to lose faith in their capabilities. They fall easy victim to stress and depression.

Self-Efficacy Take-aways

Perceived self-efficacy refers to people's belief in their capabilities to exercise control over their own functioning and over events that affect their lives. Belief in personal efficacy affects life choices, level of motivation, quality of functioning, resilience to adversity, and vulnerability to stress and depression.

Learned Optimism

In his book, *Learned Optimism: How to Change Your Mind and Your Life*, Martin Seligman draws on more than twenty years of clinical research to demonstrate how optimism enhances the quality of life, and how anyone can learn to practice it. Dr. Seligman, who is known as the father of the new science of positive psychology, offers many simple techniques for learning optimism. He explains how to break an "I give-up" habit, develop a more constructive explanatory style for interpreting your behavior, and experience the benefits of a more positive internal dialogue.

Despite equal talent and drive, optimists tend to succeed more than their pessimistic counterparts. The good news is that you can learn optimism and lean on it to respond to adversity and develop greater resilience. Through descriptions of dozens of studies performed since the 1970's, Seligman shows the benefits of optimism and describes how cognitive techniques designed to tweak your natural disposition can give you the advantage of optimism.

Research suggests that unwarranted high self-regard can lead to violent and criminal behavior. Thus, Seligman suggests that instead of pushing for high self-esteem, parents and educators should be teaching optimism.

"Explanatory style" is the way that the little voice in your head explains your circumstances to you. Your explanatory style could be keeping you in a pessimistic state and generating a belief in your own helplessness. Developing a more optimistic explanatory style can lead you out of a depressive situation. Pessimists see setbacks as perpetual, pervasive, and personal. But optimists bounce back from setbacks because they don't take them personally. Optimists expect problems to be just temporary. Pessimism derives from a deep-seated sense of helplessness. The pessimistic belief that "nothing I do matters" can become a self-fulfilling prophecy.

In laboratory experiments, "learned helplessness" had nearly the same impact and fundamentally the same cause as full-blown depression: the belief that in the face of bad or uncontrollable events, individual action does not matter. Fortunately, people can unlearn learned helplessness. In fact, unlearning this habitual reaction seems to "inoculate" people against future helplessness. Optimism gives rise to resilience. By studying people who do not give up easily or who bounce back more quickly, researchers are realizing that resilience comes down to the explanations people give themselves when things go bad.

Everyone suffers failures, but resilient people have a different reaction from those who descend into lasting depression. How personally do you take failure? How permanent do you believe it is? How pervasively does it affect your life?

Pessimists tend to believe bad things happen to them as a result of permanent causes. A pessimist may say, "You never talk to me," generalizing a particular instance of adversity into a permanent characteristic. By contrast, an optimist says, "You haven't talked to me lately," isolating a troubling event and not extrapolating it into a permanent explanation. Pessimists frequently use "always" and "never" to explain setbacks and trouble. People with an optimistic explanatory style find that good events are caused by permanent conditions, and that bad events are the result of temporary factors. An optimistic lottery winner might say, "I'm always lucky," rather than "It's my lucky day." Permanent explanations for the causes of adversity lead to helplessness; temporary explanations produce resilience.

"Pervasiveness" refers to how you allow the explanations for one setback to become explanations across a range of situations. Pessimists tell themselves that bad events will undermine their whole lives. An optimist believes good things result from pervasive reasons, while setbacks are related only to short-term circumstances. "Personalization" is an aspect of the explanatory style you use to account for bad events. Do you internalize (blame yourself) or externalize (blame others)? In this dimension, once again, the optimist internalizes good things and externalizes bad things, while the pessimist internalizes the bad and externalizes the good. Pessimistic explanatory styles turn moments of learned helplessness into full-blown depression, adding importance to the issue of hope and hopelessness. If you explain your failure to yourself pessimistically, you may then expect your future to be full of failure based on this one experience. Both drug and cognitive therapies relieve depression, but cognitive therapy gives you new ways to view old problems and to change your explanatory style. Cognitive therapy relieves depression more successfully and makes it less likely to return. It offers inoculation against future severe depression.

Learned Optimism Takeaways

- Whether you are a pessimist or an optimist depends on how you explain bad events to yourself.

- Pessimists often personalize bad life events, attributing them to permanent, pervasive causes. Yet they ascribe temporary, impersonal, specific causes to good events.

- The projection of present despair into the future causes hopelessness.

- Optimists externalize causes of adversity and see them as temporary and specific. They credit good events to personal, permanent, pervasive causes.

- Optimists are much quicker than pessimists to get over a setback and try again.

- Pessimists have one advantage over optimists: they are better at realistically assessing their situations.

- Optimists tend to exaggerate the control they have over events.

- Pessimism is a reliable predictor of depression.

- Through cognitive therapy, it is possible to change your "explanatory style" to be more optimistic.

Appreciative Inquiry Theory

David Cooperrider of Case Western Reserve University developed appreciative inquiry theory. According to Cooperrider and Whitney, appreciative inquiry theory is about the search for the best in people, their organizations, and the relevant world around them. In its broadest definition, it involves systematic discovery of what makes a living system most successful in economic, ecological, and human terms.

Appreciative Inquiry (AI) is a change management approach that focuses on identifying what is working well, analyzing why it is working well and then doing more of it. The basic tenet of AI is that an organization will grow in whichever direction that people in the organization focus their attention. The appreciative inquiry theory deliberately seeks to work from a "positive change core"—and assumes that every living system has many untapped, rich, and inspiring accounts of the positive. Linking the energy of this core directly to any change agenda mobilizes changes that were never thought possible.

Appreciative inquiry involves the art and practice of asking questions that strengthen a system's capacity to seize, anticipate, and heighten positive potential. It involves the mobilization of inquiry through the crafting of the "unconditional positive question" and often involves hundreds or even thousands of people.

Appreciative Inquiry Takeaways

- Appreciative inquiry challenges organizations to take a strengths-based approach when assessing and adapting their services or products.

- Instead of taking a problem-solving approach, appreciative inquiry offers a **possibility focus**, a move from *what is* to *what could be*.

- Based on powerful, affirmative questions, people interview each other to uncover experiences that resemble what we want to create.

Strengths Approach

The Clifton StrengthsFinder measures the presence of 34 talent themes or strengths. (Talents are people's naturally recurring patterns of thought, feeling, or behavior that can be productively applied.) The more dominant a talent theme is in a person, the greater the theme's impact on that person's behavior and performance.

In 1998, the father of Strengths Psychology, Donald O. Clifton, along with Tom Rath and a team of scientists at Gallup, created the online StrengthsFinder assessment. In 2004, the assessment's name was formally changed to "Clifton StrengthsFinder" in honor of its chief designer.

The goal of Clifton, Rath, and the Gallup researchers was to start a global conversation about what's right with people. Rath expressed that, "We were tired of living in a world that revolved around fixing our weaknesses. Society's relentless focus on people's shortcomings had turned into a global obsession. What's more, we had discovered that people have several times more potential for growth when they invest energy in developing their strengths instead of correcting their deficiencies."

Based on more than 40 years of research, the Gallup scientists created a language of the 34 most common talents and developed the Clifton StrengthsFinder assessment to help people discover and describe these talents. In 2007, building on the initial assessment and language from StrengthsFinder 1.0, Rath and Gallup scientists released a new edition of the assessment, program, and website, dubbed "StrengthsFinder 2.0." This assessment instrument has helped millions discover and develop their natural talents.

According to Rath, when you are not in your "strengths zone," you are quite simply a very different person. You may dread going to work, treat your customers poorly, achieve less on a daily basis, and have fewer positive and creative moments. Gallup's research shows that operating in your "strengths zone" improves your confidence, direction, hope, and kindness toward others.

StrengthsFinders Takeaways

- Each person's talents are enduring and unique.

- Each person's greatest potential for growth is in the area of his or her greatest strength.

- As an organization or as an individual we can:

  - Reach our maximum potential only by using our individual strengths.

  - Match our strengths to our roles at work, home, and in the community.

  - Enjoy what we are doing because we are using our true talents.

Based on these take-aways, you may take the following action steps:

- Find out what makes you stand out.

- Determine the roles in which you naturally excel.

- Invest more time in the areas where you have the most potential for greatness.

- Build on who you already are.

- Seize the opportunity to do what you do best, every day. Extraordinary growth can happen as a result.

Design Thinking

Design thinking was originally invented by Bernard Roth, a Stanford University professor, and others at Stanford as an engineering strategy to improve products and experiences. Design thinking has to be repurposed from its original intent to help individuals become happier and more successful.

In his book, *The Achievement Habit*, Roth has written about how design thinking can help a person create meaningful changes in their life. Essentially, he outlines how to stop wishing, start doing, and take command of your life.

Design thinking is a five step process:

1. Empathize. Learn what the issues are.

2. Define the problem. Which questions are we going to answer?

3. Ideate. Generate possible solutions.

4. Prototype. Abandon perfection and develop your project or your plan.

5. Test and get feedback from others.

According to Roth, while individual steps are tools, they are not as important as the guiding principles behind design thinking: a bias toward action and limited fear of failure. The point of design thinking is to challenge your automatic thinking and assumptions.

Roth boldly declares that eliminating two phrases from your vocabulary helps lead to success in life. The two phrases to eliminate are *but* and *have to*. Roth recommends replacing *have to* with *want to*, and replacing *but* with *and*. Instead of saying, "I want to go to the movies, but I have work to do," Roth suggests saying, "I want to go to the movies, and I have work to do."

When you use the word *and*, your brain begins to consider how it can deal with both parts of the sentence. For example, you might see a shorter movie or you could delegate some of the work.

Similarly, Roth recommends the simple exercise of changing *I have to* to *I want to*. This exercise is very effective in getting people to realize that what they do in their lives is in fact what they have chosen.

Both of these vocabulary tweaks are key components of design thinking. Experimenting with different language allows you to realize that a problem is not as unsolvable as it seems at first glance, and that you have more control over your life than you previously believed.

Design Thinking Takeaways

- Achievement can be learned. It is a muscle, and once you learn how to flex it, you will be able to meet life's challenges and fulfill your goals.

- Don't try—DO.

- Excuses are self-defeating.

- Believe you are a doer and achiever and you'll become one.

- Learn to resist distractions that prevent you from achieving your goals.

- Become open to learning from your own experience and from those around you.

- The brain is complex and is always working with our egos to sabotage our best intentions. However we can be mindful; we can create habits that make our lives better.

In Summary

Scientific theoretical foundations of "Positive Self-Talk" are the sum total of:

- **Self-efficacy**- one's belief in one's ability to succeed in specific situations or to accomplish a task.

- **Learned Optimism** – optimism can be cultivated by consciously challenging any negative self-talk.

- **Appreciative Inquiry** - focus on what's possible through interactive discovery and design sessions.

- **StrengthsFinders** – discover what one does best and focus on strengths.

- **Design Thinking** - a bias toward action; limiting fear of failure; and challenging automatic thinking assumptions.

What are types/categories of self-talk?

Research shows there are five specific categories of self-talk: calming/relaxing self-talk, instructional self-talk, motivational self-talk, evaluative self-talk and focus self-talk.

Calming/Relaxing Self-Talk

Calming/relaxing self-talk is intended to help you stay calm and relaxed in stressful situations.

> Examples:
>
> - "Just relax."
>
> - "Take a deep breath."
>
> - "Take it easy."
>
> - "God is in control!"
>
> - "Let me drink a glass of water."
>
> - "Let me take a walk."
>
> - "I will lie down and close my eyes for a few minutes."
>
> - "I am going to take a quick nap."

Written Activity Question - *Add Your Calming/Relaxing Self-Talk Example:*

Instructional Self-Talk

Instructional self-talk is intended to guide you to accomplish specific and complex tasks.

> Examples:
>
> - "I am going to organize my entire house one room and one item at a time."
>
> - "I am going to install this software on my laptop with the help desk guiding me step by step."

- "I will memorize all my lines for this important play one line at a time."

- "I am going to fix this dishwasher by following the troubleshooting manual."

Activity Question - Add Your Instructional Self-Talk Example:

Motivational Self-Talk

Motivational self-talk is intended to encourage you to accomplish a challenging, long, and important function that requires patience.

Examples:

- "Yes, I can do this!"

- "This TV interview is going to give me the branding exposure I want. I am going to take my time and prepare to succeed."

- "I am very well prepared and I am going to do really well!"

- "This soccer tournament is huge, and I have practiced so many times with my team as a goalie. I am going to do great!"

Activity Question - Add Your Motivational Self-Talk Example:

Evaluative Self-Talk

Evaluative self-talk asks you to reflect on events or behavior you recently completed.

Examples:

- "I just completed this important job interview and I answered most questions with confidence."

- "I did not have enough time to answer all questions. Next time, I will practice for timeliness."

- "My last two job interviews did not lead to a job offer. I did not provide sufficient examples of my accomplishments. I am going to write out examples of my significant accomplishments in preparation for my next job interview."

Activity Question *- Add Your Evaluative Self-Talk Example:*

Focus Self-Talk

Focus self-talk reminds you to concentrate on an important task that needs to be completed on time and with quality.

Examples:

- "Stay on task and return all phone calls after the task is completed."

- "Stay focused on the task and check emails after the task is completed."

- "I am going to complete my top two priority items before starting anything else."

Activity Question *- Add Your Focus Self-Talk Example:*

What does research show about the benefits of positive self-talk?

The study of self-talk, particularly in the field of sports, provides numerous studies showing the positive effects of positive self-talk on achieving performance goals. Some interesting examples are summarized below.

One relevant research project, led by psychologist Ethan Kross of the University of Michigan, studied the pronouns people use when they talk to themselves.

According to Kross, a subtle linguistic shift — shifting from "I" to your own name — can have powerful self-regulatory effects. When LeBron James, for example, talked about his decision to leave Cleveland for the Miami Heat in 2010, Koss noticed that James created distance from himself in his use of language. "I wanted to do what was best for LeBron James," the star athlete said. Kross notes that people who used "I" had a mental monologue that sounded something like, "Oh, my God, how am I going do this? I can't prepare a speech in five minutes without notes. It takes days for me to prepare a speech!" However, people who used their own names were more likely to give themselves support and advice, saying things like, "Ethan, you can do this. You've given a ton of speeches before." These people sounded more rational and less emotional — perhaps because they were able to get some distance from themselves.

Also of great interest is a meta-analysis of 32 studies on self-talk and sports performance, conducted by Hatzigeorgiadis and associates. Based on the premise that what people think influences their actions, self-talk strategies have been developed to direct and facilitate human performance. In this meta-analytic review, the researchers examined the effects of self-talk interventions on task performance in sports and possible factors that may moderate the effectiveness of self-talk. They found that self-talk interventions were more effective for tasks involving relatively fine, compared with relatively gross, motor demands, and for novel, compared with well-learned, tasks. Instructional self-talk was more effective for fine tasks than was motivational self-talk. Finally, interventions which included self-talk training were more effective than those that did not. The results of this study established the effectiveness of self-talk in sports, and encourage the use of self-talk as a strategy to facilitate learning and enhance performance.

Similarly, Eshgarf and Dana conducted an article review on the relationship between self-talk and learner proficiency level. Their analysis concluded that self-talk has a significant impact on the motor performance of beginners and skilled people.

Summary of Benefits of Positive Self-Talk

- Builds confidence: If you feel shy about addressing an audience, positive self-talk can help you overcome the fear and give you the confidence you need. People who are successful at what they do believe in themselves and their abilities.

- Controls stress: Stress negatively affects people physically, emotionally, mentally, and professionally. Using positive self-talk helps you overcome stress and remain calm.

- <u>Improves performance</u>: Through positive self-talk you can encourage yourself to accomplish the most challenging assignments.

- <u>Increases life span</u>: An optimistic view and positive self-talk contribute to a long and fulfilling life.

- <u>Increases productivity</u>: You can get more done in less time by believing in yourself and encouraging yourself.

- <u>Increases career success</u>: Through positive self-talk, you can become more productive and well-liked by your employers, bosses, and co-workers, which helps you achieve career success.

- <u>Improves health</u>: Research has found numerous health benefits to positive self-talk, including greater resistance to the common cold, decreased depression, and reduced risk of death from cardiovascular disease.

- <u>Better coping during hardships</u>: As human beings, we all have many life challenges. People who use positive self-talk are in a better position to cope with life challenges and better able to overcome setbacks in life.

Activity Question

What are the three benefits that are most important to you? Why?

What are proven strategies and techniques for improving your positive self-talk?

- **Use positive phrasing**. Tell yourself to stay cool rather than telling yourself "do not be upset."

- **Address yourself in the second person.** "You can do this, Adam." Addressing yourself in the second person helps to maintain objectivity in self-talking.

- **Surround yourself with positive people**. Ensure the people within your inner circle encourage you to achieve your goals.

- **Focus on solutions rather than dwelling on problems.** Instead of brainstorming nine reasons you lost the last contract bid, brainstorm nine actions you can take to win the next contract.

- **Strive for gratitude**. Focus on likes rather than dislikes. Example: What are five things my co-workers do well rather than dwelling on five things they need to correct.

What are practical everyday tips based on the principles of positive self-talk?

Check off which of these you practice:

_____ Always think before you speak, even jokingly.

_____ When in doubt about saying something, make positive statements about yourself and others.

_____ If you do not have nice things to say, do not say anything.

_____ If you do inadvertently say things that are not nice, do not repeat them. Get back to positive self-talk and comments.

_____ Feel free to repeat nice things you say or hear. Repetition creates absolute reality.

_____ Repeat compliments about others, but do not repeat derogatory remarks you may hear.

_____ Positive words uplift your mood. As an exercise, try looking in the mirror and speaking positive words to yourself – then watch the glow on your face.

_____ Start affirming you can accomplish your goals and stop complaining about your inability to accomplish results.

_____ Add smiles to your positive words; you look more attractive when you smile.

_____ Compliment people you encounter rather than complaining about them and watch your joy grow.

_____ Form the habit of encouraging others when they need it.

_____ In public places, randomly make eye contact with strangers and ask how they are doing with a genuine smile.

_____ When you go shopping, be sure you make eye contact, smile, and ask the cashier or salesperson, "How are you doing today?" If possible, refer to them by name (hint: look at their name tag.)

Activity Question

1. *What are other small and practical things you do or can do that are in line with positive self-talk and positive actions?*

2. *What are experiences/feelings/feedback you receive from your positive actions?*

What are strategies for eliminating or controlling negative self-talk?

- **Write in a journal** – keep a journal of your positive and negative thoughts and comments. You may keep track of when you had such thoughts; where you were; and who you were with. Keeping a journal helps you keep track of situations that trigger such thoughts or comments and examine them for improvement.

- **Thought-stopping** – As you become aware of negative thoughts, stop yourself and loudly say "stop!" This helps you become more aware of your thoughts and keep negative thoughts under control.

- **Rubber Band Snap** – keep a rubber band around your wrist, and when you become aware you are giving yourself negative self-talk, snap the band against your wrist as a self-reminder to replace the negative self-talk with positive.

Written Activity:

1. *What other techniques will you use to control using negative self-talk?*

Reframing: how do you turn negative self-talk into positive?

One key way to change negative self-talk to positive is to reframe the situation in your thoughts. Negative self-talk usually contains distortions such as exaggeration or focusing exclusively on the negative. Reframing corrects the distortions with a true thought that looks at the situation from a new angle. The chart below demonstrates this concept with examples of negative self-talk and corresponding reframed positive self-talk.

Activity: The first two rows of the chart are complete. Portions of the remainder of the chart are left blank for you to fill in.

Negative Self-Talk	Positive Self-Talk
No way I will like this.	This gives me an opportunity to try and learn something new.
This is too complicated. I am not going to master this.	I will take it one step at a time and eventually master this.
Provide an example here:	*Provide an example here:*
I have no time for this.	*Provide an example here:*
Provide an example here:	I can try to see if it works.

I am not ready for this change.	*Provide an example here:*
I will never be good at this.	*Provide an example here:*

Concluding Remarks:

Positive self-talk can be learned and developed through a process of reframing. Reframing is turning negative self-talk into positive self-talk. Given its physical, emotional, and professional benefits, positive self-talk is easy to sell. However, becoming aware of your self-talk habits, cleansing yourself of negative self-talk, and transforming to habitual positive self-talk is a long journey. With patience, time, commitment, and the application of the strategies, techniques, and tips provided in this book, you will become a full-fledged positive self-talker — a new, happier, and fulfilled self.

End of Chapter Application Activities

What is your state of negative self-talk versus positive self-talk?

What strategies/techniques/tips are you ready to adopt?

References

Bandura, A. (1993). Perceived self-efficacy in cognitive development and functioning. *Educational Psychologist, 28*(2), 117-148.

Bandura, Albert *(1997)*. Self-efficacy: The exercise of control. *New York:* W. H. Freeman.

Clifton, D. & Rath T. (2015). *How Full in Your Bucket.* Gallop Press, New York.

Cooperrider, D., & Whitney, D. (2005). *Appreciative inquiry: A positive revolution in change.* Oakland, CA: Berrett Koehler Publishers.

Eshgarf, S., & Dana, A. (2015). Review article: Self-talk and learner proficiency level. *Research Journal of Sport Sciences, 3*(7), 186-189.

Goldstein, D. (2017). Nix the negativity: Building your confidence muscle through positive self-talk. *Forbes online*, October. Found at **https://www.forbes.com/sites/forbescoachescouncil/2017/10/24/nix-the-negativity-building-your-confidence-muscle-through-positive-self-talk/#70348dc2149c**

Hardy, J. (2006). Speaking clearly: A critical review of the self-talk literature. *Psychology of Sport and Exercise, 7*(1), 81-97.

Hatzigeorgiadis, A., Nikos, Z., & Theodorakis, Y. (2011). Self-talk and sports performance: A meta-analysis. *Perspectives on Psychological Science, 6*(4), 348-356.

Kross, E., & associates. (2014). Self-talk as a regulatory mechanism: How you do it matters. *Journal of Personality and Social Psychology, 106*(2), 304–324.

Rath, T. (2007). *Strengths Finder 2.0.* Gallup Press, New York.

Roth,, B. (2015). *The Achievement Habit.* HarperCollins Publishing, New York

Seligman, M (2006). Learned Optimism: How to Change Your Mind and Your Life. Random House. NY

Seligman, M. (2011). *Flourish: A visionary new understanding of happiness and well-being.* New York, NY: Free Press.

Seligman, M. Learned Optimism Test, found at **http://web.stanford.edu/class/msande271/onlinetools/LearnedOpt.html**

Tod, D., & associates. (2011). Effects of self-talk: A systematic review. *Journal of Sport & Exercise Psychology, 33*(5), 666-687.

Zourbanos, N., & associates. (2013). The effects of motivational self-talk on self-efficacy and performance in novice undergraduate students. *Journal of Athletic Enhancement, 2*(3).

Your self-talk is the channel of behavior change.

— Gino Norris

Chapter 3

Reflective Planning
How Best to Mine Your Past to Guarantee Future Success

Selected Quotes

“ ”

Plans fail for lack of counsel, but with many advisers they succeed.

— Proverbs 15:22

A goal without a plan is just a wish.

— Antoine de Saint-Exupéry

By failing to prepare, you are preparing to fail.

— Benjamin Franklin

Without leaps of imagination or dreaming, we lose the excitement of possibilities. Dreaming, after all is a form of planning.

— Gloria Steinem

Give me six hours to chop down a tree and I will spend the first four sharpening the axe.

— Abraham Lincoln

Abstract

The beginning of a new season is a good time for planning what to accomplish in the time ahead. A new season can be a new year, a birthday, an anniversary, or a life changing situation. This chapter offers reflective planning as a friendly tool for gently reflecting on your past successes and your values in order to map out a successful future.

Reflective planning harnesses all your positive assets – values, strengths, and desired changes. To get started with reflective planning:

1) Use reflective planning templates for personal planning and organizational planning.

2) Dedicate an hour of reflective time to get started.

3) Designate a reflective planning accountability partner.

Reflective planning can guide you in setting your course of action for the next season of your life. For best results:

- Reflect on one word that describes you.

- Reflect on your proudest personal accomplishment this past season.

- Reflect on personal change you want to make this season to improve your quality of life.

- Reflect on one career change you want to make this season.

- Reflect on as many of your best attributes as you can list.

- Secure an encouraging accountability partner to help you implement your plan.

As you start reflective planning, keep in mind making your goals SMART. Are your goals specific? Are they measurable? Are they achievable? Are they relevant? Are they timely?

Reflective planning is a special planning tool to achieve success in life. Life success is guaranteed when personal interest goals and community interest goals are in good balance. Personal interest goals directly benefit you and your family. Community interest goals directly benefit your community.

Rate Your Current Level of Reflective Planning
(1=Poor, 2=Below Average, 3=Average, 4=Good, 5=Excellent)

Reflective Planning Actions	1=Poor 5=Excellent (Circle One)
1. You have personal interest goals.	1 2 3 4 5
2. You have community interest goals.	1 2 3 4 5
3. You know how to write SMART goals.	1 2 3 4 5
4. You frequently reflect on your successes in life to plan your future pursuits.	1 2 3 4 5
5. You frequently reflect on the proudest moments of your life in general.	1 2 3 4 5
6. You frequently reflect on the proudest moments of your career life.	1 2 3 4 5
7. You frequently reflect on your strengths.	1 2 3 4 5
8. You frequently reflect on the strengths of people around you.	1 2 3 4 5
9. You frequently reflect on the positive contributions people around you make to your well-being.	1 2 3 4 5
10. You frequently reflect on the positive contributions of organizations you work with.	1 2 3 4 5

Your total score is _____

Assess your score:

40 +	Outstanding
30 +	Very Good
25 +	Good
Below 25	Needs Improvement

Reflective Planning Success Story

Note: The purpose of this story is to illustrate the application of principles and skills covered in this chapter. The story is based on character elements of real people I know personally, but the details and events are my creative work designed for illustrative purposes.

Karen, Zinash, Debra, Shari, Lishan, and Missy are members of ***Women for Healthy Competition Tennis Club***. The women enjoy meeting once a week and play tennis for fun and healthy competition. They agreed to adopt three fun traditions:

> 1) The winner of a game chooses where they will have refreshments after the game.

> 2) The winner pays for refreshments for the entire team.

> 3) The winner also recommends a once a month self-development workshop of interest to the group.

During one of the Thursday games, Karen prevailed with a strong serve and she took the team to the nearest Starbucks Coffee. While they were sipping drinks they enjoyed, Zinash announced the group might benefit from attending an upcoming reflective planning webinar, hosted by Go Pro21 Community. The group agreed and signed up for the Webinar.

Natalia, Director of Webinars @ Go Pro21 Community facilitated using reflective planning to accomplish something bigger than yourself. Natalia gave attendees an assignment to email their one big reflective goal for the next year.

After attending the webinar, they all agreed to use their next meeting time to share their respective reflective goals for the year.

Here is a list of SMART and reflective goals shared by the tennis club members:

Karen: Identify one woman in need per month and spend an hour per month with each to use reflective planning to achieve their annual life goal.

Lishan: Volunteer as a technology ambassador of goodwill with Go Pro21 Community, where I will share with at least 10 random IT professionals I meet per month on using their nearest American Job Center for their career advancement needs.

Zinash: Volunteer as a healthcare ambassador of goodwill with Go Pro21 Community, where I will share with at least 10 random health professionals I meet per month on using their nearest American Job Center for their career advancement needs.

Missy: Volunteer as a stay at home mom ambassador of goodwill with Go Pro21 Community, where I will share with at least 10 random stay at home moms I meet per month on using their nearest American Job Center for their career advancement needs.

Debra: Volunteer as a college ambassador of goodwill with Go Pro21 Community, where I will share with at least 10 random college students I meet per month on using their nearest American Job Center for their career advancement needs.

Shari: Volunteer as a faith-based ambassador of goodwill with Go Pro21 Community, where I will share with at least 10 random faith-based people I meet per month on using their nearest American Job Center for their career advancement needs.

At the next monthly gathering

- they took turns to share their individual reflective planning goals.
- they decided to collaborate to hold each other accountable.
- they decided to meet on a monthly basis to monitor their progress.

During their reflective planning accountability meeting, each member reports out (a) accomplishments toward goal; (b) planned activities in the upcoming month; and (c) assistance needed from the group.

Success Story Discussion Questions

Which reflective planning goal resonates with you? Why?

Using the examples given in the success story, write your own SMART and reflective goal for the year.

SMART Goals as a Foundation for Reflective Planning

What are goals in general?

A person without a goal achieves nothing. This means in every area of our life, work, or family, a goal in life drives us to do work or take action. We need to make sure our goal is not just to be busy or occupied but to live with purpose and fulfillment.

What are Personal Interest Goals Versus Community Interest Goals

Personal interest goals are your aspirations intended to benefit you and your immediate family. Community interest goals are aspirations intended to make a difference for the community at large. Your life is complete when there is a good balance between **personal interest goals** and **community interest goals**.

Examples of Personal Interest Goals

- Complete 4 year college degree in the next five years.

- Secure 2 job promotions in the next 3 years.

- Take family vacations in different continents in the next 6 years.

- Within 3 years, acquire a family farmhouse that we will be used for farming and a weekend getaway. The farmhouse will be within an hour drive from our current residence.

Examples of Community Interest Goals

- Lead 2 economic development community organizations in the next 4 years.

- Offer 5 scholarships to needy students in the next 2 years.

- In 5 years, our organization will create 4% of good paying jobs in our immediate geographic community.

- We will contribute 1% of annual compensation of our employees toward their deferred savings for employees who will be engaged in youth mentoring in our community.

Why personal and community goals?

- Personal interest goals focus your actions so you enhance your quality of life and the qualify of life of your immediate family.

- Community interest goals are intended for the common good.

- Engaging in community Interest goals is what makes us human, makes a difference for others, and brings fulfillment for our existence.

What does S.M.A.R.T goal mean?

SMART goal refers to a method for writing goals that are clear so that you and others can easily tell when you achieve the stated goal.

SMART stand for *Specific-Measurable-Achievable-Relevant-Timely*.

Let's define each and give some examples:

SMART GOALS

Specific	Simple, Sensible, Significant In "Complete 4 year college degree in the next five years," college education and not education in general
Measurable	Meaningful, Motivating In "complete college education in 5 years," 4 year degree and not a 2 year degree
Achievable	Agreed, Attainable This goal is achievable in 5 years.
Relevant	Reasonable, Realistic & Resourced, Results Based In this example, resource availability is reasonable.
Timely	Time-Based, Time Limited, Time/Cost Limited, Timely, Time Sensitive In this example, 5 years refers to timeliness.

You Want to Practice Writing SMART Goals?

Your personal interest goals and community interest goals that are written as SMART goals have a better chance of succeeding.

In the space provided below, write your personal interest SMART goal or your community interest SMART goal.

S =

M =

A =

R =

T =

What is reflective planning?

Reflective planning is proactively thinking about future activities that will contribute to your quality of life. While reflective planning looks to the future, it is based on a self-assessment of your values, your past successes, and your best attributes.

How is reflective planning different from regular planning?

Reflective planning is a special type of planning and differs from regular planning in the following ways:

1. Reflective planning is deliberately positive.

2. Reflective planning focuses on strengths.

3. Reflective planning looks at past successes.

4. Reflective planning encourages finding an accountability partner to ensure you move forward with the planned activities that will lead to your success.

What is contained in reflective planning?

Reflective planning contains the following four elements:

1. Your personal values. (What is really important to you? Family? Career? Faith? Service to others?)

2. Your best attributes. (What are your strengths? What is your passion? What are you good at?)

3. The personal changes you want to make (your health? your income? your education?)

4. The career related changes you want to make (change profession? skills upgrade?)

What are key activities in conducting reflective planning?

The first step is to reflect on and identify one positive word that describes you.

The second key activity is evaluating and recording what you value most. This may be one or more items. You may identify the one thing that you value the most or describe your proudest life accomplishment as an indicator of your top value.

Third, write down personal changes you wish to make. What is your top priority for change – the amount of time you spend on electronic devices? your eating habits? your pattern of spending? your health? Reflect on what matters most to you.

Fourth, document a career improvement action. What is your top priority action item to improve your professional life?

Fifth, recall and record your best attributes as indicated by your success journey. What is your claim to fame? What is one thing you are known for? What is one word that your friends and colleagues use to positively describe you? (Remember, we are not talking about any negative attributes – think positive!)

Sixth, brainstorm your life mission statement. Think through your purpose in life. This step is where you link your best attributes to positive societal outcomes such as human rights, child welfare, environmental justice, and job creation.

Seventh, enlist an accountability partner to help you put your reflective plan into action. This final step is crucial to make your plan a reality.

How do you maintain fulfillment and excitement in reflective planning?

Traditional planning is a heads down, step by step process that is not usually associated with positive fulfillment and excitement-produced energy. One way to ensure positive fulfillment and excitement is to link reflective planning to societal impacts and payoffs.

Roger Kaufman of Florida State University has been a pioneer in linking individual and organizational activities to societal outcomes and payoffs. Here is Kaufman's prescription for considering societal payoffs: "Society as primary client is both sensible and practical. Every day we all depend on other organizations, public and private to put our safety, survival and quality of life first on their agenda. We depend on all organizations with which we deal each and every day, such as airlines, public transport, cars, supermarkets, food processors, drug manufacturers, and energy suppliers, to assure that our safety and well-being will be first and foremost on their agenda. It is on ours."

The final question on each of the planning templates below asks you to identify societal impact. Use your imagination to address this question and maximize the energy and sense of fulfillment from the planning exercise.

Example of a completed personal reflective plan:

Below is a summary of one family's personal reflective planning.

Reflective Planning Questions	MA	ME	EM
1. What is one word that describes you?	Perseverance	Generous	Empathetic
2. What is your proudest personal accomplishment this past year?	Got my first degree	Started middle school	Selected to join school symphonic orchestra
3. What personal change do you want to make this year to improve your quality of life?	Be more comfortable with self	Help people more	Do things for others more/service
4. What one career change do you want to make this year?	Find entry level job or internship in my field	Get things done on time	Energy & time management
5. What are your positive attributes?	Helpful, smart, skillful, problem solver, servant leader	Funny, silly, smart	Kind, generous, smart, funny, loving, positive, like spending time with family, considerate, dramatic
6. What is your personal mission statement? What is your purpose in life?	Encourage other girls to succeed	Encourage people to be themselves	Show people their self-worth

Example of an organizational reflective plan:

Below is a summary of the organizational reflective planning session of a work team with inputs from individual team members.

Reflective Planning Questions	UM	BF	AN
1. When you think of your organization, what is one word that comes to mind?	Adaptable	Responsive	Teamwork
2. Describe one success story that your organization accomplished this year?	Developed regional leadership teams	Continued to attract "top talent"	Passed regulatory agency audit with flying colors
3. What is one action that your organization must take to get to the next level in the upcoming year?	Standardize organizational internal processes	Build a strong infrastructure to support new business and sustain growth	Systems - create more systems/standard procedures and processes
4. What do you expect to accomplish as a member of your organization in the upcoming year?	Implement sustainable growth strategy	Build the Recruiting Team to support new and currently awarded contracts	Serve as a catalyst for career improvement for area communities
5. What are your organization's best attributes?	Customer focused, collaborative, flexible	Supportive, team-oriented, entrepreneurial	Caring, positive, flexible
6. What is one contribution that your organization must make to the communities it is part of?	Create good paying jobs in our communities	Aid underserved communities with our skill sets	Create local jobs

What are the essential techniques of personal reflective planning?

Worksheet for personal reflective planning:

The following are strategic questions to help you reflect on your core values and best attributes. This exercise will be most helpful if you devote some time to reflecting on the questions and write your answers in the space provided. Better yet, do this exercise in a facilitated session with your accountability partner.

What is one positive word that describes you?	*(Answering this question helps you identify one positive trait that represents you.)*
What is your proudest personal accomplishment this past year?	*(Answering this question connects you with what you really value in life.)*
What personal change do you want to make this year to improve your quality of life?	*(Answering this question helps you prioritize and focus your attention on a personal change that improves your quality of life.)*
What is one career-related change you want to make to improve your professional life?	*(Answering this question helps you identify a career improvement action plan.)*
What are your positive attributes?	*(Attributes refer to your passion and your strengths. Your best attributes are your assets for success. Answering this question gives you the confidence to succeed.)*
What is your personal mission statement/What is your purpose in life?	*(To help answer this question, consider articulating your purpose in life. Why are you here on earth?)*

Worksheet for organizational reflective planning:

These questions are intended for members of your organizational planning group, which may consist of the leadership team or a work team. Summaries of each team member's responses serve as inputs to your organization's planning process.

When you think of your organization, what is one word comes to mind?	*(Responses to this question discover the value and vision of the organization.)*
Describe one success story that your organization accomplished this year?	*(Responses to this question identify the accomplishments the team is proud to report out.)*
What is one action your organization must take to get to the next level?	*(Responses to this question identify strategic priority actions.)*
What do you expect to accomplish as a member of your organization this year?	*(Responses to this question identify your contributions to the team.)*
What are your organization's best attributes?	*(Responses to this question identify the hidden and intangible assets that will help propel your organization to future success.)*
What is one contribution that your organization must make to the communities you are part of?	*(Responses to this question identify the difference our work makes to the society we live it.)*

Practice Activity

Incorporating SMART Goals into Reflective Planning

In the reflective planning templates previously provided, identify and mark items that may be written using SMART goals. This book belongs to you, and you have the author's authority to write on it and mark up when SMART Goals must be incorporated.

In the template provided below, write your general mission statement and then re-write the statement in SMART format. Discuss this with your accountability partner and update your statement.

Your General Mission Statement	SMART Mission Statement
Example Context: Let's say you are a 25-year-old American, and you want to become president of the USA. Your general mission statement may read something like this:	*Smart Goal Example* I want to serve my country and my people in elected office to inspire my people to be at peace with themselves and with others. In other words, my mission is to inspire my people to feel fantastic about themselves and feel even more fantastic about others.

| I want to become President of the United States. | By the time I turn 60, I want to be elected President of the United States.

When I turn 50, I want to be elected as a member of Congress.

When I turn 40, I want to be elected as governor of my home state.

Over the next 10 years (age 25 to 35), I will make 10 million diverse friends on social media.

. |

When should reflective planning occur?

The best occasions for launching reflective planning are as follows:

Seasonal Option 1:
At the start of a new year – this may be your New Year's resolution.

Seasonal Option 2:
At the start of a special season such as a new fiscal year, new school year, new football season, etc.

Seasonal Option 3:
At the start of a regular lunar season (spring, summer, fall, and winter.)

Seasonal Option 4:
At the start of a personal life event – your birthday; new job or promotion; just married; first child born; just retired, etc.

Once you choose your preferred seasonal option, stick with it. The true value of reflective planning comes from doing it repeatedly.

How often should reflective planning be updated?

Again, reflective planning is most beneficial if you review and update it frequently and regularly. Here are possible planning cycles:

Minimum Cycle:
For reflective planning to have value, at a minimum you must do it once a year with a check up each quarter.

Better Cycle:
A better practice is to conduct reflective planning on a quarterly basis with a monthly checkup.

Optimal Cycle:
Ideally, you will conduct reflective planning on a monthly basis with a weekly checkup. This option yields the best outcome.

Written Activity:

Why does the optimal monthly/weekly planning cycle yield the best outcome?

What are the benefits of reflective planning?

1. Helps you make decisions by realizing and articulating what you value most.

2. Helps you identify your strong attributes to prepare you for new opportunities.

3. Helps you identify changes that will move you to the next level of your career.

4. Helps you identify personal changes to improve your quality of life.

What are the best implementation strategies for reflective planning?

While establishing your reflective plan in writing is the first step, implementing the plan is an equally important next step. There are three important implementation strategies:

1. Make a public announcement
The first step in implementing reflective planning is making a public announcement of your planned action steps. Making a public announcement…

1) creates outside pressure for you to follow through with your plan;

2) allows you to get commitment and help from family and friends;

and 3) allows you to get useful suggestions and feedback to improve the plan.

2. Designate an accountability partner
The second step in implementing reflective planning is designating an accountability partner. This is a person (or persons) who will cheer you on as well as hold you to accomplishing the commitment you made.

A good accountability partner is (1) willing to play the role; (2) available to meet with you on regular basis; and (3) able to balance encouraging you and holding you accountable.

3. Periodic checkups
The third step in implementing reflective planning is periodic checkups to determine and modify action steps. These regular checkups keep your plan

useful and moving forward. While conducting checkups is your responsibility, your accountability partner can help with inputs and insights.

Concluding Remarks

Reflective planning harnesses all your positive assets – values, strengths, and desired changes. To get started with reflective planning:

> 1) Use reflective planning templates for personal planning and organizational planning.
>
> 2) Dedicate an hour of reflective time to get started.
>
> 3) Designate a reflective planning accountability partner.

Reflective planning can guide you in setting your course of action for the next season of your life. For best results:

- Reflect on one word that describes you.

- Reflect on your proudest personal accomplishment this past season.

- Reflect on personal change you want to make this season to improve your quality of life.

- Reflect on one career change you want to make this season.

- Reflect on as many of your best attributes as you can list.

- Secure an encouraging accountability partner to help you implement your plan.

As you start reflective planning, keep in mind making your goals SMART. Are your goals specific? Are they measurable? Are they achievable? Are they relevant? Are they timely?

Reflective planning is a special planning tool to achieve success in life. Life success is guaranteed when personal interest goals and community interest goals are in good balance. Personal interest goals directly benefit you and your family. Community interest goals directly benefit your community.

End of Chapter Activity

Who is your accountability partner for your reflective planning activity? _____

When do you plan to complete your reflective planning session?

What season? _____

Date _____   *Time* _____

Location _____

Reflective Planning Questions	Self	Accountability Partner
What is one word that describes you		
What is your proudest personal accomplishment this past year		
What personal change do you want to make this year to improve your quality of life?		
What one career change do you want to make this year?		
What are your positive attributes?		
What is your personal mission statement/What is your purpose in life?		

References

Berg, J (2015) Frontiers in Psychology. The Role of Personal Purpose and Personal Goals in Symbiotic Visions

Kaufman, R., & Watkins, R. (2003). *Strategic planning for success: Aligning people, performance and payoffs.* New York, NY: John Wiley & Sons.

Whitaker, R. (December 2015) Harvard Study- Smart Goals and You.

https://aboutleaders.com/harvard-study-smart-goals-and-you/#gs.oalwYpQ

https://www.ncbi.nlm.nih.gov/pmc/articles/PMC4396129/

> *If you don't know where you are going, you'll end up someplace else.*
>
> — Yogi Berra

Chapter 4

Generosity

How Your Giving Makes a Difference

Selected Quotes

One gives freely, yet grows all the richer; another withholds what he should give, and only suffers want.

— Proverbs 11:24

Judge not, and you will not be judged; condemn not, and you will not be condemned; forgive, and you will be forgiven; give, and it will be given to you. Good measure, pressed down, shaken together, running over, will be put into your lap. For with the measure you use it will be measured back to you.

— Luke 6:37-38

Whoever is generous to the poor lends to the LORD, and he will repay him for his deed.

— Proverbs 19:17

The remarkable bottom line of the science of love is that giving protects overall health twice as much as aspirin protects against heart disease.

— Stephen Post

You give but little when you give of your possessions. It is when you give of yourself that you truly give.

— Kahlil Gibran, *The Prophet*

"A fight is going on inside me," said an old man to his son. "It is a terrible fight between two wolves. One wolf is evil. He is anger, envy, sorrow, regret, greed, arrogance, self-pity, guilt, resentment, inferiority, lies, false pride, superiority, and ego. The other wolf is good. He is joy, peace, love, hope, serenity, humility, kindness, benevolence, empathy, generosity, truth, compassion and faith. The same fight is going on inside you. The son thought about it for a minute and then asked, "Which wolf will win? The old man replied simply, "The one you feed."

—Wendy Mass, Jeremy Fink and the Meaning of Life

Abstract

Acts of generosity make our world a better place. If we all only look out for ourselves and our own kind, our world will be a miserable place. Giving time and being emotionally generous can be as valuable as giving money. Acts of generosity make a difference in the lives of recipients whether the recipients are individuals or organizations or communities. There is extensive research that demonstrates the benefits of generosity to the giver. For example, one of the notable researchers on generosity, Dr. Stephen Post writes, "The remarkable bottom line of the science of love is that giving protects overall health twice as much as aspirin protects against heart disease." Post reports that giving to others has been shown to increase health benefits in people with chronic illness including HIV, multiple sclerosis, and heart problems.

According to Adam Grant, Wharton professor and author of *Give and Take*, people fit into one of three reciprocity styles. Givers like to give more than they get, paying attention to what others need. Takers like to get more than they give, seeing the world as a competitive place and primarily looking out for themselves. Finally, matchers balance and give on a quid pro quo basis, willing to exchange favors but careful about not being exploited.

Grant argues that givers are actually the most successful of the three types. Givers build larger, more supportive networks; they inspire the most creativity from their colleagues; and they achieve the most successful negotiations. Givers find ways to grow the pie and take their share of it.

If you wish to fine tune your acts of generosity, here are a few basic actions that you may add to your bag of generosity tools:

- Think generous.

- Start small.

- Focus your acts of generosity in your areas of passion.

- Create space for generosity by systematically scaling back your material possessions.

Rate Your Current Level of Generosity
(1=Poor, 2=Below Average, 3=Average, 4=Good, 5=Excellent)

Generosity Actions	1=Poor 5=Excellent (circle one)
1. Your acts of generosity includes taking care of yourself by taking care of your spiritual and emotional needs.	1 2 3 4 5
2. You spend time with people in need.	1 2 3 4 5
3. You give first from what you earn before you start spending it.	1 2 3 4 5
4. You intentionally seek to own less material possessions.	1 2 3 4 5
5. You understand your success is more than your material possessions.	1 2 3 4 5
6. You spend time considering the needs of others.	1 2 3 4 5
7. You are content with your current material possessions.	1 2 3 4 5
8. You readily give emotional lift to the people around you.	1 2 3 4 5
9. You believe what and when you give makes a difference.	1 2 3 4 5
10. You are engaged in a volunteer activity that makes a difference for others.	1 2 3 4 5

Your total score is _____

Assess your score:

40 +	Outstanding
30 +	Very Good
25 +	Good
Below 25	Needs Improvement

Generosity Success Story

Note: The purpose of this story is to illustrate the application of principles and skills covered in this chapter. The story is based on character elements of real people I know personally, but the details and events are my creative work designed for illustrative purposes.

Jenny is a very busy woman. She is Deputy Chief Financial Officer of a human capital consulting firm. She is also volunteer Director of Refreshments and Love for a cross cultural community organization, where she leads a team of volunteers to ensure every community meeting's refreshments are served with love and joy. Jenny makes sure her Refreshments & Love committee members demonstrate love and joy during their time of public service as well as during their internal meetings. Jenny also serves on the membership committee of the PTA of her daughter's school. In this role, Jenny quietly dedicates at least 5 hours a week to update and maintain the member database of the school PTA. In addition, Jenny serves on the logistics and administration team of the local Bible Study Fellowship (BSF). In this capacity, she makes time on a weekly basis to meet with one of the BSF volunteers for coffee and fellowship. Jenny is a mother of two daughters, where she believes her mission is to provide the love and support they need while growing up. She is also happily married to a CEO of a growing business and a community leader who supports her purpose driven activities.

Despite her multiple roles, Jenny takes her dual roles of wife and mother as her most important and primary duties. Jenny creatively makes time for all her important responsibilities. In her own words, here is how Jenny is able to balance all her responsibilities with incredible ease and composure:

"My number one criteria for choosing what I do is to answer one question:

Does this make a difference? I only do things that make a difference. Working on things that I believe make a difference gives me positive energy."

"Every activity has a task side and a relationship side. I quietly perform the task side with full attention and with a great attention to details. My secret to getting things done is to perform a task as early as possible." Her husband and daughters are always in awe of Jenny's ability to quietly and quickly get the most challenging work done.

"I make time for the relational side of work by making one-on-one time with the people I work with. Relationships are developed one-on-one. I spend quality time with my husband, daughters, family, and friends. With one-on-one time, I learn and receive energy. I also ask what I can do to help the person."

"I constantly express gratitude for the opportunity to engage with important activities that make a difference and for all the people in my life."

Jenny uses four secrets to fulfill her numerous obligations: (1) she more heavily relies on her scheduling app than on caffeine; (2) she deliberately tries to balance out all her obligations; (3) she focuses on the personal touch; and (4) in all things, she tries to focus on the big prize.

Short Story Discussion Questions

How do you rate Jenny's level of generosity? Explain.

Given Jenny's hectic schedule, what else can she do to improve her acts of generosity?

Generosity defined

Generosity is defined as the intention and act of giving to benefit the recipient. To understand the true essence of generosity, it is helpful to look at the visible and invisible aspects of giving.

The visible part is the act of giving, which includes gifts that are transferred from the giver to the receiver in the form of money, possessions, time, attention, encouragement, emotional availability, prayers, kindness, talents, experiences, lessons learned, and the like.

The invisible aspect of generosity is the attitude and intention behind the act of giving. If the giver is offering gifts based on the true needs and for the well-being of the recipient, the act qualifies as true generosity.

What is emotional generosity?

Emotional generosity is a special form of generosity. It is the act of giving positive emotions to others without expecting anything in return. Emotionally generous people continuously bring happiness, love, and positivity to others. They love praising others, rewarding people, recognizing the talents of others, showing signs of appreciation, and other actions that spread positive emotions.

What are the motives of generosity?

Notre Dame sociologist Christian Smith, coauthor of the recent book *The Paradox of Generosity*, notes that scholars have yet to prove that altruistic acts come from selfish motives, such as the paradoxical expression "to give is to receive." Based on a survey of thousands of Americans, Dr. Smith found that "humans are not just rational egoists out to maximize their own prestige, power, or wealth." Instead, the survey showed that generosity depends to a large degree on a person's perception of "living in a world of abundance, blessing, gratitude, enjoyment, security, and sharing." Those who see the world as threatening or full of scarcity give less even though they have a similar financial ability to give.

Nature's Testimony on the Virtue of Giving: The Tale of Two Seas

There are two lakes in Israel: the Sea of Galilee and the Dead Sea. Both lakes are attached to and fed by the Jordan River. The Sea of Galilee takes the water from the Jordan River and then feeds it back to the river and other streams. The Sea of Galilee is the lake that nourishes most of Israel; it is filled with life, and in turn, it also gives life to many.

The Dead Sea, on the other hand, though also fed by the Jordan River, does not feed anything and keeps all the water it is given. The Dead Sea is barren and lifeless. Any life that tries to live in it dies. There are other lakes around the world that also only receive and do not give, resulting in only death.

What research studies show the benefits of generosity?

While generosity is intended to directly benefit the recipients of the giving, the unintended beneficiaries of giving are the givers themselves.

In an article titled, "Generous people live happier lives," in the July 2017 *Science Daily*, neuro-economists from the University of Zurich found that generosity makes people happier, even if they are only a little generous. People who act solely out of self-interest are less happy. Merely promising to be more generous is enough to trigger a change in our brains that makes us happier.

The benefits of generosity are well summed up by the title of a book co-authored by Dr. Stephen Post, one of the leading authorities on generosity. *Why Good Things Happen to Good People: How to Live a Longer, Healthier, Happier Life by the Simple Act of Giving* says it all.

Dr. Stephen Post is a bioethicist at Case Western Reserve University and founder of the Institute for Research on Unlimited Love. The idea for this center was suggested to him by Sir John Templeton, grantmaker and zealous advocate of the interplay between science and religion. Since 2001, Post has explored the extraordinary power of giving by funding over 50 studies at 44 major institutions. This research has focused on the traits and qualities that create happiness, health, contentment, and lasting success in life.

Post writes: "The remarkable bottom line of the science of love is that giving protects overall health twice as much as aspirin protects against heart disease." Post reports that giving to others has been shown to increase health benefits in people with chronic illness including HIV, multiple sclerosis, and heart problems.

The astounding new research includes a fifty-year study showing that people who are generous during their high school years have better physical and mental health throughout their lives. Other studies show that older people who give live longer than those who are less generous, and that people of all ages who help others on a regular basis, even in small ways, feel happiest.

In a 2013 article, "Generosity and the Maintenance of Marital Quality," Dew and Wilcox examined whether generosity in marriage was associated with marital quality. They found that generosity – defined here as small acts of kindness, displays of respect and affection, and a willingness to forgive one's spouse his or her faults and failings – was positively associated with marital satisfaction and negatively associated with marital conflict and perceived divorce likelihood. This is the first study to test the relationship between generosity and marital quality and it found that both receiving and extending marital generosity is associated with higher quality marriages among married couples age 18 to 45 in the United States.

Happify.com is a website devoted to providing science-based pathways to greater happiness. Research cited there shows that those who helped friends, relatives, or neighbors, or gave emotional support to their spouses had a lower risk of dying over a five year period than those who did not.

In one study, participants were asked to spend five dollars on themselves or five dollars on someone else. Those who spent on others were measurably happier. Research also shows that experiential gifts lead to more happiness than material ones. Experiential gifts include: vacations, lessons such as art, music, or cooking, memberships to gyms, museums, or botanical garden, and tickets to an event.

Smith and Davidson, in *The Paradox of Generosity*, convincingly show that self-reports of generosity are strongly associated with various good outcomes.

Whether measured as tithing (giving away a percentage of one's annual income), volunteer hours, or acts of "relational" kindness to friends and neighbors, generosity appears to coincide with happiness, good health, avoidance of depression, a sense of purpose in life, and a sense of personal growth.

Nicholas Christakis, formerly of Harvard University and now at Yale, has undertaken a variety of studies on the link between generosity and social networks. According to Christakis, if people never behaved generously or altruistically toward one another, social ties would dissolve and the networks around us would disintegrate. Thus, generosity is "crucial for the emergence and endurance of social networks. Moreover, once networks are established, altruistic acts – from random acts of kindness to organ donation – can spread through them."

According to a study led by Professor Dae Hee Kwak, seeing an organization donate to charity may cause individuals to want to donate as well. In this study, when participants felt more grateful for their team's donation, they also were more likely to want to donate to the charity themselves.

Research by Whillansa and Dunna shows that prosocial giving (voluntary actions that are intended to help or benefit another individual or group of individuals) lowers blood pressure. The researchers looked at the relationship between prosocial spending or giving money to others and blood pressure, a simple measure of cardiovascular health. One hundred eighty-six adults who had been diagnosed with high blood pressure were asked to indicate how much money they spent on charities and other causes, and then followed up with two years later. By then, the participants who had initially spent the most on causes had lower blood pressure than participants who had spent less money. This association held even after accounting for the effects of income, education level, and age.

According to Adam Grant, Wharton professor and author of *Give and Take*, people fit into one of three reciprocity styles. Givers like to give more than they get, paying attention to what others need. Takers like to get more than they give, seeing the world as a competitive place and primarily looking out for themselves. Finally, matchers balance and give on a quid pro quo basis, willing to exchange favors but careful about not being exploited.

Grant argues that givers are actually the most successful of the three types. Givers build larger, more supportive networks; they inspire the most creativity from their colleagues; and they achieve the most successful negotiations. Givers find ways to grow the pie and take their share of it.

Summary of the benefits of generosity:

As shown above, researchers from multiple disciplines have demonstrated abundant benefits of generosity. A partial list of benefits include:

- Improved sense of well-being

- Lower stress

- Lower blood pressure

- Reduced depression

- Better physical health

- Greater marital satisfaction

- Enhanced emotional health

- Enriched sense of purpose in life

- Increased happiness

- Longer life

How generous is America as a nation?

I have a personal testimony to share about American generosity. First, let me admit: I was not born in America. I am a native of Ethiopia and lived in Ethiopia until adulthood. I now live in America as a naturalized citizen and identify myself as Ethiopian-American.

While still living in Ethiopia, I attended a unique high school with a diverse faculty from America and other major countries. All the teachers were good in their subjects, but generally our relationship was transactional – knowledge was transferred.

In contrast, our relationship with the American teachers was relational. The American teachers gave us time, friendship, attention, warmth, and encouragement. They were emotionally and personally involved in our learning and our well-being, and they were by far the most generous and giving teachers.

I recall receiving a gift of shoes from one of my American PE teachers. I also vividly remember when our American history teacher, Mr. George, finished his assignment and returned to America. The entire school chartered buses to go to the airport to send him off with tears and love. The entire summer after Mr. George left us, it felt like losing an uncle. Due to these positive and generous experiences with our high school teachers, my fellow students and I all fell in love with America.

Today, I am still in love with America. I believe the reason America is so blessed with innovation, ingenuity, and wealth is due to its generosity toward people around the world. In my experience, Americans are the most generous people on earth.

For example, my study leading to a Ph.D. degree in Instructional Systems Design from Florida State University was fully paid for by American taxpayers, for which I am eternally grateful. At every opportunity, I express gratitude to groups of fellow Americans at various venues when the subject of generosity comes up.

I am happy to report that my personal experience with American generosity is not an isolated case. Studies show that America is a generous nation; in fact, numerous studies rank Americans as the most generous people on Earth. According to the organization Giving USA, in 2014 Americans donated almost $360 billion to charity, the highest total in the report's 60-year history.

My Tribute to America as a Nation of the Most Generous People: What Makes America Very Very Special?

Background

Generosity is not a lone behavior. It exists with other virtuous behaviors. In other words, generous people possess other prosocial behaviors such as decency, genuine curiosity, seeing good in others, and optimism.

I wrote this tribute on the most recent Christmas morning as my gift of love to America.

America is very very special. Through the eyes of an immigrant, who likes to reflect and who tries to look deeper, the following are special characteristics of America as I have come to know it.

1) The American people are abundantly generous. When I first arrived in America over 30 years ago as a foreign student, my American classmates were eagerly willing to help me with my school work and invited me to their homes for meals. My classmate Pat invited me to her family Thanksgiving dinner, where I learned her husband Melvin did all the cooking. I believe showing generosity to complete strangers is a very American trait because I have witnessed and benefitted from Americans with diverse political, religious, and ethnic backgrounds.

2) The American people are exceptionally decent, which is expressed in kindness, class, and fairness. I was recently having lunch with my friend John, and I asked him to bless the food assuming he was of a Christian faith. He complied quietly. Toward the end of our meal, John asked me if I knew he was an atheist. The decency with which John expressed himself is characteristically American and a mark of decency in action.

3) The American people are genuinely curious. Because of my Ethiopian-English accent, the most common question I receive is where I am from. What ensues is always a pleasant and curious conversation about another nice Ethiopian they know of or willingness to know more of my version of the Ethiopian story.

4) The American people see the good in others. My wife and I noticed one of our Bible study teachers, Mike, leads discussions where he affirmatively acknowledges whatever viewpoints are expressed. In my household, we coined the term *Mikeism* to remind each other to acknowledge and respect every

viewpoint expressed by others.

5) The American people are absolutely optimists. As a college football fan (proud Florida State Seminole), I watch every game when my team has a fabulous season. I see lots of fans who sport their team jersey and invest their time and money in going to live sports games regardless of the seasonal performance of their teams. The mindset of supporting their losing team with a faith that their team will have a winning season the next time around is so American and a mark of optimism.

Yes, on the surface, there are obvious divides along political, religious, ethnic, and educational lines. There are even more superficial differences along the lines of vegetarians vs. meat lovers, shoppers vs. non-shoppers, etc.

However, at a deeper level, the Americans people are:

- Tremendously generous
- Exceptionally decent
- Genuinely curious
- See the good in others
- Absolutely optimists

What do generous people have in common?

They see more to give than money:

Generous people have much more to offer this world than financial resources. They are personally involved in their giving and offer time, talents, experience, and lessons learned.

Generous people think beyond their money and begin to invest their lives in others. Often this step is more difficult than signing a check. That is why this is the number one characteristic of generous people.

In addition, generous people possess the following characteristics:

- Altruism: Generous people give freely and without expecting to receive compensation for their good deeds.

- Optimism: Generous people believe that their giving is going to make a difference.

- Trust: Generous people trust in the causes they support and in the people that are involved in those causes.

- Energy: Generous people bring tremendous energy to the causes they support. In return, they are further energized by their causes.

- Contentment: Generous people are content with their possessions and thus willing to spend more on their causes._

- Emotional generosity: Generous people give positive emotions to others without expecting anything in return. They love praising others, rewarding people, recognizing the talents in others, showing signs of appreciation, and other similar actions.

- Own less and give away more: Generous people live a more minimalist life. They intentionally decide to own less. Living a minimalist life does not automatically make you a more generous person, but it provides the space necessary to make it possible. With less stuff in your life, you will have more money, time, and energy to help others. And the intentionality that emerges in your life will help you discover the need for generosity.

What is the latest in the changing landscape of philanthropy?

During the Thanksgiving week of 2015, the Chief Executive of Facebook, Mark Zuckerberg, and his wife, Priscilla Chan, announced their plan to eventually donate 99 percent of their Facebook stock. This announcement marks the changing landscape of philanthropy. Why?

- The amount of money donated is one of the largest ever (this is a commitment of $45 billion US dollars.)

- The donors are among the youngest to make this commitment (early 30's.)

- The commitment was made in the most personal manner – in a Facebook posting addressed to their newborn baby girl, Max. The couple have made it clear the donation is inspired and motivated by the birth of their first born baby.

- The funds were committed to such causes as fighting disease, improving education, and building strong communities.

- While typical philanthropy donations are made to non-profit organizations, this funding commitment was made to a profit and nonprofit hybrid initiative, the Chan Zuckerberg Initiative, to be under the control of the donor couple.

While this particular announcement – given the timing, motivation, and magnitude of the donation – is worth the attention it has attracted, the trend of increasingly large sums of money given to charity has been underway in recent years.

Here are some other recent philanthropy-related events:

- The world's wealthiest business leaders seem to be challenging each other to give away their fortunes before they die. Recently, Zuckerberg joined Bill Gates and a number of others to boost clean-energy and climate research.

- In 2010, Gates and Warren Buffett publicly launched the Giving Pledge to encourage billionaires to donate the bulk of their wealth to charity.

- More than 130 billionaires worldwide have joined them.

- Among them is Judy Faulkner, founder of electronic health records company, Epic, who reportedly said she plans to give away 99 percent of her money.

- Saudi Prince Alwaleed bin Talal, one of the richest men in the world, said the pledge inspired him to eventually give away his entire fortune, more than $30 billion.

Recent social science research shows that self-made billionaires are bigger philanthropists than those who inherit their wealth. Self-made billionaires are four times more likely to have signed the giving pledge than billionaires who inherited their money. There are two possible explanations for this interesting finding: (1) One explanation is that self-made billionaires want their children to grow up to be self-reliant like them. So there might be psychological reasons why self-made billionaires want to give away more of their money to philanthropy. (2) It's also possible that self-made people are simply more confident about making money, so they have less hesitation about giving it away and spending it because they know they can always go out and make some more.

Here is what this development and trend says about philanthropy and about generosity:

- Generosity is a positively contagious act. It is fun to watch these wealthy folks out-give each other.

- Generosity is an overwhelming emotion and act. Once the generosity bug affects a person, there is no limit to their giving level.

- Generosity is a privilege that defies categorization to any age group, nationality, or religious group. For that matter, it defies wealth level.

If stories of generosity are inspiring to hear, they are even more enriching and fulfilling when practiced first hand.

How do you improve your generosity level?

One online resource to help build the generosity culture is Happify.com (http://my.happify.com/).

Happify.com (http://my.happify.com/public/science-behind-happify/) summarizes the science behind their website as follows:

1. Our brains can be changed, even when we are adults.

2. The pathway to change is adopting new thought patterns, training our brain as if it were a muscle, to overcome negative thoughts.

3. All of us are hard-wired for negativity, but we can profoundly benefit from learning new ways to react and deal with everyday stresses.

4. It doesn't take a lot of effort to make a real difference in your life. A few simple and even entertaining mental diversions will change things.

Although some people are more generous by nature than others, everyone can learn to be more giving. And learning about how generosity makes a difference for people in need and also has many positive consequences for givers can motivate us to increase our level of giving.

In *American Generosity: Who Gives and Why*, Patricia Snell Herzog and Heather E. Price offer two important tips to advance generosity

1. **Talk About Your Giving**: In order to increase giving feel free to talk about your own giving without bragging. This inspires others to give more

2. **Present Impacts of Giving**: Fundraisers and development professionals use this technique to appeal to the various giver types. For example, planned givers, as part of their systematic approach, value feedback about "what their donations accomplished" from the organizations to which they donate.

Whether you want to give more to benefit others or yourself, below are some ways to become more generous.

1. <u>Start small</u>: Start your journey toward generosity by giving something small. It may be giving a dollar to a community cause or giving a smile to all the people around you for an hour a day. Giving a smile does not cost anything, and it will improve your own mood while lifting up someone who may need it.

2. <u>Give what feels comfortable to give</u>: Do not give out of obligation or beyond your means.

3. <u>Embrace gratitude</u>: Spend more time thinking about what you already possess and less time thinking about what you do not have. Expressing gratitude frees you up to consider the needs of others, and you are apt to give more.

3. <u>Give first</u>: When you receive your next check, give before you start spending. If you wait until you have leftover money, there may be none. So, give before you start spending on your own needs.

4. <u>Redirect one specific expense to giving</u>: It may be skipping the Saturday movie or an expensive daily coffee. Do not go overboard and make it fun and memorable.

5. <u>Find a cause based on your passion</u>: Figure out what you are passionate about. Child nutrition? Public health? Clean environment? Eliminating hunger? Give time or money to your cause.

6. <u>Spend time with people in need</u>: Spending time with people in need gives you firsthand experience and helps you see the commonalities among all people.

7. <u>Live a more minimalist life</u>: Intentionally own less so that you can consider others with more needs.

8. <u>Practice being generous to yourself</u>: Take care of yourself not only materially but spiritually and emotionally. Allow yourself time to relax, enjoy a hobby, spend on your health and well-being. Also, acknowledge yourself for the difference you are making in the world.

9. <u>Give your stuff away</u>: Once a year, go through your clothes, books, and other household items and donate what you no longer use. You can also ask around and see if anyone you know needs those items.

10. <u>Show kindness</u>: When you see a mom struggling to keep a door open while maneuvering a stroller through it, take a minute to grab the door for her. When you notice someone's smile or cute hairstyle, tell them. When you walk by someone, say hello. It is so easy to stay in our own busy world, but simply showing kindness can change someone's day.

11. <u>Ask how you can help</u>: If you go to an event at your child's school, stay for a few minutes afterward to help clean up. If there is a working lunch at your office, help throw the trash away before you go back to your cubicle. At the end of a long day, everyone appreciates hearing, "How can I help you?" It is such a simple thing and doesn't cost a dime!

12. <u>Share your talents</u>: How can you use your talents to give to others? Brainstorm a list of things you could do for people by using your natural abilities. You might love organization; could you help a friend who struggles in that area (and who has asked for help)? If you know how to play an instrument, you could give lessons as a gift to someone. If you love to cook, there are always new moms who would so appreciate a home-cooked meal.

Concluding Remarks

Acts of generosity make our world a better place. If we all only look out for ourselves and our own kind, our world will be a miserable place. Giving time and being emotionally generous can be as valuable as giving money. Acts of generosity make a difference in the lives of recipients whether the recipients are individuals or organizations or communities.

Givers are more successful than non-givers. Givers build larger, more supportive networks; they inspire the most creativity from their colleagues; and they achieve the most successful negotiations. Givers find ways to grow the pie and take their share of it.

If you wish to fine tune your acts of generosity, here are a few basic actions that you may add to your bag of generosity tools:

- Think generous.

- Start small.

- Focus your acts of generosity in your areas of passion.

- Create space for generosity by systematically scaling back your material possessions.

End of Chapter Activity

(1) What is one act of generosity that you recently witnessed? Who were the actors? What was the outcome?

(2) List and describe the top 3-5 generosity acts you currently practice?

(3) How do you plan to improve your current state of generosity? List specific action steps below:

Examples:

> *(a) During my daily train commute, I will make eye contact with complete strangers and smile at least six times per day.*

> *(b) I will skip my daily large macchiato drink once a week and donate the funds to the United Way. I will take a walk after lunch (when I would otherwise be drinking the macchiato) to improve my cardio functioning.*

References

Americans donated an estimated $358.38 billion to charity in 2014. (2015, June 29). *Giving USA*. Retrieved from http://givingusa.org/giving-usa-2015-press-release-giving-usa-americans-donated-an-estimated-358-38-billion-to-charity-in-2014-highest-total-in-reports-60-year-history/

Becker, J. 10 little ways to become more generous. *Becoming Minimalist*. Retrieved from http://www.becomingminimalist.com/10-simple-ways-to-become-a-more-generous-person/

Christakis, N., & Fowler, J. (2014, March 23). Social networks and the spread of altruism. Retrieved from http://kindness-is-contagious.com/social-networks-spread-altruism/

Chua, C. Are you emotionally generous? Retrieved from http://personalexcellence.co/blog/emotional-generosity/

Dew, J., & Bradford Wilcox, W. (2013). Generosity and the maintenance of marital quality. *Journal of Marriage and Family, 75*(5), 1218-1228.

The Giving Institute. Found at http://www.givinginstitute.org/

Goers, A. (2012, November 13). How to be generous when you do not feel like it. *Balanced Mind and Soul*. Retrieved from http://balanceinme.com/blog/how-to-be-generous-when-you-do-not-feel-like-it/

Grant, A. (2013). *Give and Take: Why Helping Others Drives our Success*. Penguin Random House.

Happify. Found at http://my.happify.com/

Hardwick, B. Better Together Lessons on Life, Leadership & Faith. The Tale of Two Seas. Found at http://bryanhardwick.com/the-tale-of-two-seas/

Hergoz, P. & Price, H. (2016). *American generosity: Who gives and why*. University of Oxford, London.

Hill, C. (2015, June 16). Americans are the most generous people in the world. *MarketWatch*. Retrieved from http://www.marketwatch.com/story/americans-are-the-most-generous-people-in-the-world-2015-06-16

Jennie. (2015, January 14). How to give generously when you don't have a dime. *Little Girl Designs*. Retrieved from http://www.littlegirldesigns.com/how-to-give-generously/

wak, D & Kwon, Y. Can an organization's philanthropic donations encourage consumers to give? The roles of gratitude and boundary conditions. *Journal of Consumer Behavior*, July/August 2016. Volume 15, Issue 4

Meaux, E. 5 qualities of generous people. Gaiam Life. Retrieved from http://life.gaiam.com/article/5-qualities-generous-people

st, S., & Neimark, J. (2008). *Why good things happen to good people: How to live a longer, healthier, happier life by the simple act of giving.* New York, NY: Broadway Books.

ience of Generosity Initiative, The University of Notre Dame. Found at http://generosityresearch.nd.edu/

ne science of happiness. Found at http://my.happify.com/public/science-of-happiness/

nith, C., & Davidson, H. (2014). *The paradox of generosity: Giving we receive, grasping we lose.* Oxford University Press.

niversity of Zurich (2017). *Science Daily*, Generous People Live Happier Lives. Found at https://www.sciencedaily.com/releases/2017/07/170711112441.htm

hillansa, A. & Dunna E. Is spending money on others good for your heart?

We make a living by what we get. We make a life by what we give.
— Winston Churchill

Chapter 5

Gratitude

How Expressing Gratitude Reaps You Abundant Joy & Happiness

Selected Quotes

Feeling gratitude and not expressing it is like wrapping a present and not giving it.

— William Arthur

It's not happiness that brings us gratitude; it's gratitude that brings us happiness.

— Unknown.

Do not spoil what you have by desiring what you have not; remember that what you now have was once among the things you only hoped for.

— Epicurus

This is the day that the Lord has made; Let us rejoice and be glad in it.

— Psalm 118:24

Gratitude can transform common days into thanksgivings, turn routine jobs into joy and change ordinary opportunities into blessings.

— William Arthur Ward

Be thankful for what you have; you'll end up having more. If you concentrate on what you don't have, you will never, ever have enough.

— Oprah Winfrey

True happiness is to enjoy the present, without anxious dependence upon the future, not to amuse ourselves with either hopes or fears but to rest satisfied with what we have, which is sufficient, for he that is so wants nothing. The greatest blessings of mankind are within us and within our reach. A wise man is content with his lot, whatever it may be, without wishing for what he has not.

— Seneca

Abstract

Gratitude is a feeling of appreciation or thanks for what an individual receives that may be tangible or intangible. Research shows that people who practice gratitude reap the benefits of improved physical health, more positive emotions, more relish of good experiences, improved ability to deal with adversity, stronger relationships, increased energy, increased optimism, and increased empathy.

Regardless of how well you rate yourself in practicing gratefulness now, practice will increase your gratitude and expressing it will become more natural. As you become a more grateful person, your return on investment will keep increasing.

Some tips for improving acts of gratitude include:

- Maintain a daily gratitude journal.

- Send periodic thank you letters to people who made a difference in your life.

- Keep a happiness jar – accumulate notes of happiness moments for occasional referral at a future date.

- Exchange "your joyous moment of the day" with family, friends, colleagues, and acquaintances.

The more you practice gratitude, the more attuned you are to it and the more you can enjoy its psychological benefits. A recent brain scanning study found that people's brains are still wired to feel extra thankful even months after a short gratitude writing task. The implication is that gratitude tasks work, at least in part, because they have a self-perpetuating nature.

Rate Your Current Level of Gratitude

(1=Poor, 2=Below Average, 3=Average, 4=Good, 5=Excellent)

Gratitude Actions	1=Poor 5=Excellent (circle one)
1. You readily thank family members for who they are as well as what they do for you and what they do for others.	1 2 3 4 5
2. You frequently thank your colleagues for their contributions as well as for who they are.	1 2 3 4 5
3. You thank your direct reports, protégés, children, etc., for their accomplishments and for their efforts.	1 2 3 4 5
4. You often thank your friends for their friendship as well as for what they do for you and what they do for others.	1 2 3 4 5
5. You express gratitude for what your organizational leaders accomplish and for their efforts.	1 2 3 4 5
6. You often express gratitude to the customers who buy your services and products.	1 2 3 4 5
7. You readily thank people in places where you buy products and receive services from others.	1 2 3 4 5
8. You readily thank casual acquaintances for their accomplishments and their efforts.	1 2 3 4 5
9. You readily express gratitude to people you communicate with virtually including emails, texts, and phone conversations,	1 2 3 4 5
10. Your prayers contain more praise and worship and less requests and demands for your benefit and for the benefit of your loved ones.	1 2 3 4 5

Your total score is _____

Assess your score:

40 +	Outstanding
30 +	Very Good
25 +	Good
Below 25	Needs Improvement

Gratitude Success Story

Note: The purpose of this story is to illustrate the application of principles and skills covered in this chapter. The story is based on character elements of real people I know personally, but the details and events are my creative work designed for illustrative purposes.

Kiddy is a hospital Chief Operations Officer. One day, Kiddy's 6-year-old daughter, Yana, asked Mom to spend a day with her watching what she does and how she does it. Mom agreed and they decided to do job shadowing on a Friday that Yana was out of school.

On the way to work, Kiddy and Yana stopped at Panera Breads to grab breakfast. Yana noticed that Mom thanked the store manager who served them for rolling up his sleeves and serving side by side with his staff. After they left Panera, Yana asked that they stop by the nearby convenience store to buy gum.

As they picked up their mother-daughter favorite, minty gum, Yana announced "Mom, I'm paying for this from from my allowance." Kiddy said, "I'm very grateful to be the mother of the most considerate daughter."

When the pair arrived at the office at 7 a.m., they bumped into the cleaning crew near the restroom. Kiddy told John, a cleaning crew member, "Thank you for keeping such a clean and healthy building. You are doing a very good job of keeping our staff, patients, and visitors healthy."

Mom settled in the office and checked her email with Yana watching over her shoulder. Yana asked about the first email. Kiddy explained it was a carbon copy of an email from one of their suppliers to their accounts payable complaining about an invoice which was 90 days past due.

Mom called the vendor and thanked them for supplying them with all electronic devices and servicing them in a timely manner. "We appreciate your patience and understanding as they have staff turnover in accounts payable which caused the delay. How about we pay your next three months invoices within a week?"

Immediately after the call, Rodriguez, the deputy COO walked in for their weekly huddle. Kiddy preempted the meeting and started by thanking Rodriquez for attending a hospital administrator's conference in her place and doing a great job of presenting at the conference panel for which he had little time to prepare. "Rodriguez, you are my reliable partner."

Later, Kiddy and Yana joined Susan, the hospital CEO, for lunch. After they ordered lunch, Susan offered to pay, and Yana surprised the adults by offering to contribute tips and dropping $5 in the tips box. Yana thanked Mom and Susan for allowing her to hang out with the two most powerful women in the building. Kiddy said, "Yana, thank you for making me proud of your generosity." Susan declared to the mother and daughter, "Thank you both for making my day. Kiddy, you are responsible for making our hospital the best place to work. And, Yana, you are the most responsible 6-year-old I have ever met."

Success Story Discussion Questions

Which of the moments of gratitude impressed you the most? Why?

How does Kiddy's parenting style translate into her leadership style?

What is gratitude?

Gratitude can be broadly defined as a general state of thankfulness and/or appreciation for what is valuable and meaningful to oneself. Technically speaking, gratitude is the positive emotion one feels when another person has intentionally given (or attempted to give) one something of value. For centuries, scholars have believed gratitude is essential for building and preserving social relationships; so much so that Cicero called gratitude "not only the greatest of virtues, but the parent of all others."

What do scientific research studies show as the benefits of gratitude?

Science says gratitude is good for your health

More and more researchers are finding that gratitude is good for your health. "Clinical trials indicate that the practice of gratitude can have dramatic and lasting effects in a person's life," said Robert A. Emmons, professor of psychology at UC Davis. "It can lower blood pressure, improve immune function and facilitate more efficient sleep."

One recent study from UC San Diego's School of Medicine found that people who were more grateful actually had better heart health, specifically less inflammation and healthier heart rhythms.

New research is starting to explore how gratitude works to improve our mental health

Is gratitude beneficial for people who struggle with mental health concerns? And, if so, how?

Wong, et al report that gratitude writing can be beneficial not just for healthy, well-adjusted individuals, but also for those who struggle with mental health concerns.

In fact, it seems, practicing gratitude on top of receiving psychological counseling carries greater benefits than counseling alone, even when that gratitude practice is brief.

Being grateful improves your chances of success, studies show

Not only does gratitude help boost general well being, it also specifically improves self-esteem.

A 2014 study published in the *Journal of Applied Sport Psychology* found that athletes who were more grateful had higher self-esteem, which has been linked to higher job performance.

Expressing gratitude to subordinates pays off

A research study conducted by Grant and Gino demonstrated that a supervisor's expressed gratitude to subordinates for a job well done makes employees feel a strong sense of self-worth and confidence. The study also revealed that being grateful has a ripple effect, leading to an increase in trust between colleagues.

Write down what you are grateful for

Another study showed that participants who kept gratitude journals exercised more regularly, reported fewer physical symptoms, felt better about their lives as a whole, and were generally more optimistic about the upcoming week compared to their negatively focused counterparts.

Even a single act of kindness can go a long way

Scientists studying positive psychology found that a one-time act of thoughtful gratitude produced an immediate 10% increase in happiness and 35% reduction in depressive symptoms. The happy effects disappeared within three to six months, which shows that gratitude is an act to be repeated again and again.

It's never too early to start practicing gratitude

Psychologist and researcher Jeffrey Froh created and implemented a gratitude curriculum for kids aged 8 to 11. The youngsters who received the lessons showed an increase in grateful thinking, appreciation, and positive emotions as compared to the classmates who did not.

The lessons had long-lasting effects, with differences between the two groups at their greatest five months after the program.

Grateful schools are happy schools

Practicing gratitude increases students' positive emotions and optimism, decreases their negative emotions and physical symptoms, and makes them feel more connected and satisfied with school and with life in general. This is the result of two additional studies – suggesting gratitude should be a focus for students year round.

Fostering gratitude in schools

A study by Froh and Bono showed that when students are thankful, they feel more connected to their schools and teachers. Froh and Bono have been among the first researchers to study gratitude among youth. Since starting their research program in 2006, they have worked with thousands of children and adolescents across the United States (and now expanding to Australia, Britain, Japan, and Singapore.) Their research has shown that "gratitude does more than just make kids feel good; it also improves their mood, mental health, and life satisfaction, and it can jumpstart more purposeful engagement in life at a critical moment in their development, when their identity is taking shape."

Froh and Bono have also found that teens who had high levels of gratitude when entering high school had less negative emotions and depression and more positive emotions, life satisfaction, and happiness four years later when they were finishing high school. They also had more hope and a stronger sense of meaning in life. Another Froh and Bono study, which followed students over six months, showed that feeling grateful motivates adolescents to help others and use their strengths to contribute to society.

Applying Gratitude – Case Study of Cheryl Sandberg

Sandberg's 2016 New Year's resolution was "write down three joyful moments each day." On Facebook, Sandberg wrote, "I will try to focus on finding joy in the mundane and the profound – joy in the small things that make my children smile, joy in the moments of friendship that might otherwise pass by unnoticed, joy in the ability to appreciate the gift of life in a way I never did before."

In May 2015, Cheryl Sandberg lost her husband Dave Sandberg in a sudden treadmill accident during their family vacation in Mexico. Sandberg posted "When I first lost Dave, I felt overwhelmed with just getting through each day. My friend, Adam Grant, suggested that every night before bed I write down three things I did well that day. I tried to do this, although some days I had such a hard time thinking of anything I did well that I'd end up listing 'Made a cup of tea.' But over time, focusing on things I'd done well helped me rebuild my confidence."

Gratitude can boost a romantic relationship

While being grateful is good for you, being on the receiving end of it can do wonders for your romantic relationships! A recent study found that after receiving gratitude, participants noticed that their partner was more responsive to their needs and overall more satisfied with their relationship. Gratitude was shown to have a long-term effect that was seen six to nine months later.

Counting blessings contributes to well-being in daily life

Two researchers, Emmons and McCullough, examined the effects of a grateful outlook on psychological and physical well-being such as moods, coping behaviors, health behaviors, physical symptoms, and overall life appraisals. Results suggest that a conscious focus on blessings may have emotional and interpersonal benefits.

Gratitude increases happiness and decreases depressive symptoms

In an extensive experiment, Seligman and associates tested five gratitude activities, referred to as happiness interventions. They found that the interventions increased happiness and decreased depressed symptoms.

Here is an overview of the five activities tested:

1. Gratitude visit. Participants were given one week to write and then deliver a letter of gratitude in person to someone who had been especially kind to them but had never been properly thanked.

2. Three good things in life. Every night for one week, participants were asked to write down three things that went well that day. In addition, they were asked to write down the cause of each good thing.

3. You at your best. Participants were asked to write about a time when they were at their best and then to reflect on the personal strengths displayed in the story. They were told to review their story once each day for a week and to reflect on the strengths they had identified.

4. <u>Using strengths in a new way</u>. Participants were asked to take inventory of character strengths online at www.authentichappiness.org and to receive individualized feedback about their top five ("signature") strengths. They were then asked to use one of these top strengths in a new and different way every day for one week.

5. <u>Identifying signature strengths</u>. This exercise was a shortened version of the one just described, without the instruction to use signature strengths in new ways. Participants were asked to take the survey, to note their five highest strengths, and to use them more often during the next week.

The results were straightforward. Doing the exercises increased happiness and decreased depression, and the effects were strongest and longest lasting for those who continued the exercises on their own.

Gratitude facilitates prosocial behavior

A study by Bartlett and Desteno examined the relationship between gratitude and prosocial behavior (the opposite of antisocial behavior). Prosocial behavior refers to voluntary actions that help another individual or group of individuals. Examples include sharing, comforting, and rescuing others. Bartlett and Desteno showed that gratitude increases participants' efforts to assist others who have helped them, even when such efforts are costly. Gratitude also can increase assistance provided to strangers.

A grateful heart is a nonviolent heart

Five studies conducted by Nathan Dewall and associates support the hypothesis that gratitude is an antidote to aggression. Gratitude motivates people to express sensitivity and concern toward others and to behave compassionately toward uninvolved third parties. After studying over 900 undergraduates, Dewall concludes, "Gratitude is an equal opportunity emotion that causes lower levels of aggression."

Summary of the benefits of gratitude

Researchers from multiple disciplines show abundant benefits of gratitude. A partial list includes:

- Better health

- Increased happiness

- Reduced depressive symptoms

- Better romantic relationships

- Better coping behavior

- More positive emotions

- Better sleep

- Stronger immune systems

- Less aggression.

Additional benefits, based on my own experience, include:

- When you are grateful, others like to be around you. Your appreciation includes and supports them.

- Great resources and partners are attracted to you when they feel appreciated for who they are and what they bring to the party.

- Your relationships with family and friends are more likely to be loving and supportive when you express your gratitude for all that they bring to your life.

- Gratitude feels wonderful. It is like a warm emotional light, shining within you to banish greed, bitterness, selfishness, jealousy, envy, meanness – all the most limiting and corrosive emotions.

Activity Question - *How has gratitude benefitted you?*

What do grateful people have in common?

Grateful people possess the following common characteristics:

- Grateful people tend to be happy people.

- Grateful people count their blessings in their daily life.

- Grateful people feel a sense of abundance in their lives.

- Grateful people appreciate the contributions of others to their well-being.

- Grateful people recognize life's small pleasures.

- Grateful people acknowledge the importance of experiencing and expressing gratitude.

- Grateful people express sensitivity and concern for others.

- Grateful people are more peaceful and less aggressive toward others.

Activity Question - What is your experience with a person you consider to be super grateful?

How do you cultivate a growing sense of gratitude?

Some people are more grateful than others by nature. Learning how gratitude improves our quality of life can motivate everyone to improve their level of gratitude. Here are some gratitude activities to try:

1. Start with a gratitude session. How do you pick up this habit? So much of our life is spent in unconscious mental habits. Without noticing it, we complain, we nitpick, we stress about little faults, we see the bad in people and situations. Changing this is not going to happen immediately. But you can change a little at a time. Start with a small gratitude session, and really be thankful. Feel the happiness that something or someone is in your life. Take a moment to make a list, right now, of the things in your life you're thankful for. You just might be looking back on this moment years later, as the moment your entire life changed.

2. Maintain a gratitude journal. Write down positive things that happen to you. This slowly changes the way you perceive situations.

3. Notice new things you are grateful for every day.

4. Keep a happiness jar – drop in notes identifying things and situations you are grateful for. Read through the notes occasionally.

5. Send a gratitude letter to someone who made an impact in your life.

6. Send thank you notes – acknowledge those who have helped you.

7. Pay attention to life's positives – this will train you to see more and more of them, which will help you learn to be more grateful.

8. Share your most joyous moment of the day with family members.

Concluding Remarks

Gratitude is a feeling of appreciation or thanks for what an individual receives that may be tangible or intangible. People who practice gratitude reap the benefits of improved physical health, more positive emotions, more relish of good experiences, improved ability to deal with adversity, stronger relationships, increased energy, increased optimism, and increased empathy.

Regardless of how well you rate yourself in practicing gratefulness now, practice will increase your gratitude and expressing it will become more natural. As you become a more grateful person, your return on investment will keep increasing. Some tips for improving acts of gratitude include:

- Maintain a daily gratitude journal.

- Send periodic thank you letters to people who made a difference in your life.

- Keep a happiness jar – accumulate notes of happiness moments for occasional referral at a future date.

- Exchange "your joyous moment of the day" with family, friends, colleagues, and acquaintances.

The more you practice gratitude, the more attuned you are to it and the more you can enjoy its psychological benefits. A recent brain scanning study found that people's brains are still wired to feel extra thankful even months after a short gratitude writing task. The implication is that gratitude tasks work, at least in part, because they have a self-perpetuating nature.

End of Chapter Activity

1. *What is your most joyous moment of the last 24 hours?*

2. *What are 5 events in your life today for which you are grateful?*

3. *What are 5 events in your life in general for which you are grateful?*

4. *What are some gratitude techniques that you would like to incorporate into your future journey of gratitude?*

(Examples: Once a week, send a thank you letter to someone who made a difference in my life. Or, before going to bed every day, write in my journal three things for which I am grateful.)

References

5 scientific facts that prove gratitude is good for you. (Nov 2013). *Goodnet: Gateway to Doing Good.* Found at http://www.goodnet.org/articles/5-scientific-facts-that-prove-gratitude-good-for-you

Abauta, L. (2013, September 9). Change your state of mind with a gratitude session. Retrieved from http://lifehacker.com/change-your-state-of-mind-with-a-gratitude-session-1278856276

Bartlett, M., & Desteno, D. (2006). Gratitude and prosocial behavior: Helping when it costs you. *Psychological Science, 17*(4), 319-325. Retrieved from http://greatergood.berkeley.edu/images/application_uploads/Bartlett-Gratitude+ProsocialBehavior.pdf

Campbell, E. (2013, November 18). Grateful schools, happy schools. *Greater Good.* Retrieved from http://greatergood.berkeley.edu/article/item/grateful_schools_happy_schools

DeWall, C., Lambert, N., Pond, R., Kashdan, T., & Fincham, F. (2012). A grateful heart is a nonviolent heart: Cross-sectional, experience sampling, longitudinal, and experimental evidence. *Social Psychological and Personality Science, 3*(2), 232-240.

Dunn, L. (May 2017). *Today: Science & Health.* Be thankful: Science says gratitude is good for your health. Found at **https://www.today.com/health/be-thankful-science-says-gratitude-good-your-health-t58256**

Emmons, R., & McCullough, M. (2003). Counting blessings versus burdens: an experimental investigation of gratitude and subjective well-being in daily life. *Journal of Personality and Social Psychology, 84*(2), 377–389. Retrieved from http://www.breakthroughhealing.org/Documents/GratitudeStudy2003.pdf

Froh, J., & Bono, G. (2012, November 19). How to foster gratitude in schools. *Greater Good.* Retrieved from http://greatergood.berkeley.edu/article/item/how_to_foster_gratitude_in_schools

Grant, A., & Gino, F. (2010). A little thanks goes a long way: Explaining why gratitude expressions motivate prosocial behavior. *Journal of Personality and Social Psychology, 98*(6), 946–955.

Jarrett, C. (January 7, 2016). How Expressing Gratitude Might Change Your Brian. Science of Us.

Knickerbocker, R. Prosocial behavior. *Learning to Give.* Retrieved from http://www.learningtogive.org/resources/prosocial-behavior

Kindelan, K. (December 30, 2015). Cheryl Sandberg Reflects on Loss of Husband, Sets New Year's Resolution in Facebook Post. ABC News Post

http://abcnews.go.com/US/sheryl-sandberg-reflects-loss-husband-sets-years-resolution/story?id=35994513

Lyubomirsky, S. (2013). *The myths of happiness: What should make you happy, but doesn't, what shouldn't make you happy, but does*. New York, NY: Penguin Press

Ravenscraft, E. (2015, June 22). Avoid "hedonic adaptation" by breaking routines to stay happy. Retrieved from http://lifehacker.com/avoid-hedonic-adaptation-by-breaking-routines-to-stay-1713018774

Seligman, M., & associates. (2005). Positive psychology progress: Empirical validation of interventions. *American Psychologist, 60*(5), 410-421.

Seligman, M. (2011). *Flourish: A visionary new understanding of happiness and well-being*. New York, NY: Free Press.

Ward, M. (Nov 2017). *CNBC Make it*. Being grateful improves your chances of success, studies show. Found at https://www.cnbc.com/2016/11/04/being-grateful-improves-your-chances-of-success-studies-show.html

Wong, J. & Brown, J. (June 2017). *Greater Good Magazine*. How gratitude changes you and your brain. Found at **https://greatergood.berkeley.edu/article/item/how_gratitude_changes_you_and_your_brain**

> *The hardest arithmetic to master is that which enables us to count our blessings.*
>
> — Eric Hoffer

Chapter 6

Networking

How Making Connections Generates Limitless Possibilities

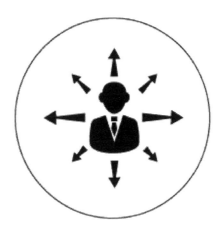

Selected Quotes

" "

I've learned that people will forget what you said, people will forget what you did, but people will never forget how you made them feel.

— Maya Angelou

Whoever isolates himself seeks his own desire; he breaks out against all sound judgment.

— Proverbs 18:1

Live in harmony with one another. Do not be proud, but be willing to associate with people of low position. Do not be conceited.

— Romans 12:16

It occurs to me that our survival may depend upon our talking to one another.

— Dan Simmons, *Hyperion*

The successful networkers I know, the ones receiving tons of referrals and feeling truly happy about themselves, continually put the other person's needs ahead of their own.

— Bob Burg

The mark of a good conversationalist is not that you can talk a lot. The mark is that you can get others to talk a lot. Thus, good schmoozers are good listeners, not good talkers.

—Guy Kawasaki

Poverty, I realized, wasn't only a lack of financial resources; it was isolation from the kind of people that could help you make more of yourself.

— Keith Ferrazzi

Abstract

Networking is making friends at your every interaction with others. Networking is strengthening your existing relationships and making new positive relationships.

The networking framework answers five basic questions: *What? Who? Why? When? How?*

- *What* is the principal content of networking? The principal content of networking is a personal story including: everyone's stories, your story, and my story.

- *Who* are the key actors in networking? Participants of networking include: everyone, you, and me. There are no spectators in networking.

- *Why* does networking matter? Networking creates human connections; it allows learning about others; it helps us learn about ourselves.

- *When* is networking most appropriate? Networking is most appropriate: when we first meet and greet; during the first part of an important meeting; and in a meeting dedicated to learning about and practicing networking.

- *How* is networking best implemented? Networking is best implemented through: personal storytelling, active listening; reciprocation; and keen observation.

General benefits of networking include:

- Forming strategic partnerships

- Gaining access to expertise

- Testing the viability of ideas

- Sharing knowledge

- Creating opportunities

- Increasing visibility.

Some strategies of networking are:

- When you are around people, unplug from electronic communication devices and tune in to the people around you.

- At events, sit next to complete strangers.

- When you meet people, convey friendliness with a generous smile, Also, repeat and learn their names.

- Highlight what you have in common, be curious to learn about people you meet, and remember to strategically brag about your accomplishments.

- Ask *why* questions when you hear people expressing views you do not agree with.

There are four networking muscles that you can develop to help you become a pro at networking:

1) Develop the habit of friendly greetings.

2) Prepare and practice presenting your elevator speech to convey a consistent message about yourself.

3) Regularly play networking bingo as practice for naturally learning personal attributes of people you meet.

4) Actively participate in speed networking to help you expand your circle of contacts.

Networking is the most powerful interpersonal skills you can use to accomplish your personal interest goals as well as your community interest goals. The more you learn and practice networking, the more effective you become and the more it works for you.

Rate Your Current Level of Networking: How robust is your networking?
(1=Poor, 2=Below Average, 3=Average, 4=Good, 5=Excellent)

Networking Actions	1=Poor 5=Excellent (circle one)
1. While networking, you unplug from electronic devices.	1 2 3 4 5
2. When attending professional meetings, you choose to sit next to people you do not know.	1 2 3 4 5
3. You point out what you have in common with others.	1 2 3 4 5
4. You engage in strategic bragging when the opportunity presents itself.	1 2 3 4 5
5. When you do not agree, you ask more *why* and *how* questions rather than immediately engaging in debate.	1 2 3 4 5
6. When you meet people, you pay attention to their names and try to remember them.	1 2 3 4 5
7. After a professional meeting, you follow up by delivering what you promised.	1 2 3 4 5
8. During conversations, you are totally focused on the person. No multi-tasking.	1 2 3 4 5
9. When you meet people you express warmth with smiles and friendly gestures.	1 2 3 4 5
10. In networking conversations, you make personal connections by trying to learn more about the person than simply what they do.	1 2 3 4 5

Your total score is _____

Assess your score:

40 +	Outstanding
30 +	Very Good
25 +	Good
Below 25	Needs Improvement

Networking Success Story

Note: The purpose of this story is to illustrate the application of principles and skills covered in this chapter. The story is based on character elements of real people I know personally, but the details and events are my creative work designed for illustrative purposes.

At a recent Go Pro21 Community Big Event, James conducted an interactive workshop on making business networking second nature. James is one of the co-founders of Go Pro21 Community, a certified coach, expert on human capital development, and owner of a training and development company.

As part of the networking activity, James asked the group to give a 30 second elevator speech answering three quick questions: (1) one word that best describes you; (2) your claim to fame or what you are known for; and (3) your life purpose.

Here is the elevator speech of each of the attendees:

Todd: one word = faithful. My claim to fame is to provide wisdom. My life purpose is to empower people to fulfill their God-given purpose in life.

Gabe: one word = cheerful. My claim to fame is to get it done without excuses. My life purpose is to be a cheerleader for those who are making a difference.

Jenny: one word = accommodating. My claim to fame is to excel at something I have not done before (run the marathon, Black Belt). My life purpose is to help others where needed.

El Shaddai: one word = hardworking. My claim to fame is to be an uplifter. My life purpose is to solve the big problems.

Negassi: one word = endurance. My claim to fame is to be strategic. My life purpose is to advocate for fairness.

Sew: one word = nice. My claim to fame is to be a truth teller. My life purpose is to make a difference in the lives of people.

Solomon: one word = respectful. My claim to fame is to go out of my way to accommodate needs of people. My life purpose is to inspire people to advance.

Lishan: one word = love, as in love for all people. My claim to fame is to speak my mind. My life purpose is to make people happy.

Tatta: one word = social. My claim to fame is easily making friends. My life purpose is helping people during their times of need.

Mekdes: one word = diligent. My claim to fame is poetic expressions. My life purpose is to advocate for social justice.

Haimy: one word = observant. My claim to fame is to understand and solve problems. My life purpose is to generate ideas to solve problems.

Martha: one word = gratitude. My claim to fame is to explore human abilities. My life purpose is to inspire people to maximize their God-given dreams and live them.

Binny: one word = peacemaker. My claim to fame is to reconcile people who have differences. My life purpose is to bring understanding among people.

Jeremy: one word = improver. My claim to fame = if it is not broken, keep trying. My life purpose = service above self

Urgessa: one word = detail oriented. My claim to fame = deliver what is committed. My life purpose = make a difference by quickly uncovering solutions to a problem.

Thomas: one word = honest. My claim to fame = enjoy advising people who are experiencing transition. My life purpose = helping people make better decisions through assessment of options with an open mind.

Kone: one word = reliable. My claim to fame = historical analysis. My life purpose = community capacity building.

Abay: one word = composure. My claim to fame = good with children. My life purpose = find simple solutions for complex problems.

Bisrat: one word = compassion. My claim to fame = strive to meet the needs of others. My life purpose = to use my full potential to make a difference.

Clarence: one word: personable. My claim to fame = establishing career in HR. My life purpose = help and support others in their career & life efforts.

Anaji: one word = helpful. My claim to fame = look forward to improving. My life purpose = using listening as a vehicle to find common ground among different people.

Tammy: one word = servant. My claim to fame = after delivering best in class service in corporate environments for over 25 years, I am now the president of TLC Enterprise, LLC, which expands my platform as a servant leader. My life purpose = change agent living a fruitful life of passion, purpose, and integrity while always looking for creative and productive ways to motivate and empower others to reach their full potential.

Abdela: one word = cautious. My claim to fame = seek to understand purpose of initiative before making any commitments. My life purpose = respect and protect the rights of people to be themselves.

Worku: one word = sociable. My claim to fame = artist expressions. My life purpose = helping people meet their needs.

Bushi: one word = diligent. My claim to fame = Never give up; keep trying until done. My life purpose = to respect other people's differences and their opinion if it is different from mine.

Tesfaye: one word = trusted. My claim to fame = influencing others. My life purpose = encouraging others.

Behailu: one word: go-getter. My claim to fame = being considered an overachiever. My life purpose = engineer and develop intelligent systems and solutions that make the lives of humans easier.

Tom: one word = curious. My claim to fame = I have made a career of learning complex subjects and then sharing my knowledge in easily understandable ways. My life purpose = to inform and educate others, particularly in the workplace.

Success Story Discussion Questions

Which elevator speech resonated with you? Why?

Using examples given above, write your brief elevator speech, including:

1. What is an animal or object or word that best describes you and why?

2. What is your claim to fame?

3. What is your life purpose?

What is networking?

Networking is the process of extending yourself to other people to exchange ideas, insights, resources, encouragement, referrals, and interests.

Networking may be informal or formal. Informal networking can take place wherever you meet people. Formal networking is a planned activity where all participants come prepared to take part in the exchange.

Networking is making friends at your every interaction with others. Networking is strengthening your existing relationships and making new positive relationships.

Overview of the the Networking Framework

The networking framework answers five basic questions: *What? Who? Why? When? How?*

What? What is the principal content of networking?	The principal content of networking is a personal story including: everyone's stories, your story, and my story.
Who? Who are the key actors in networking?	Participants of networking include: everyone, you, and me. There are no spectators in networking.
Why? Why does networking matter?	Networking matters because it creates human connections, it allows learning about others, and it helps us learn about ourselves.
When? When is networking most appropriate?	Networking is most appropriate when we first meet and greet, during the first part of an important meeting, and in a meeting dedicated to learning about and practicing networking.
How? How is networking best implemented?	Networking is best implemented through personal storytelling, active listening, reciprocation, and keen observation.

The Networking Framework Explained

What? What is the principal content of networking?	The principal content of networking is a personal story including: everyone's stories, your story, and my story.

The principal content of networking is a personal story. What actually takes place in networking is personal storytelling. I get to tell my story. You get to tell your story. We all get to tell our stories.

My top three favorite networking questions that prompt personal storytelling are:

1) what is your joyous moment of the last 24 hours?

2) what is the story behind your name?

3) Who is one of your favorite family members and why?

The joyous moment question is the most basic and appropriate when there is very limited time to network. The storytelling associated with this question relates to an event of the last 24 hours. One of the frequent joyous moment stories I hear is the story of the joy of reconnecting with a family member or a family friend or a long time friend.

For example, at a recent meeting I moderated, I asked, "what is your joyous moment of the day?" I vividly remember Tom, one of the meeting attendees, was the most joyous person to respond to the question.

Tom announced that "the day was super joyous because after 25 years of separation, I have been reunited with my sisters." The sisters that Tom referred to were Ruth and Bethlehem, who were at the same meeting. The non-verbal joy that Tom, Ruth, and Bethlehem expressed was priceless and memorable. While Ruth and Bethlehem are family friends and I see them quite often, I met Tom that day for the first time. Since then, whenever I see Tom at other social functions, I receive the friendliest greeting from Tom, and he happily repeats the joyous story all over again.

The reason behind asking the joyous moment question and related happiness questions is to create positive energy. Everyday, I ask this question to an average of 12 people per day, 360 people per month, and 4,320 people per year. This means, I hear at least an average of 12 joyous stories a day, 360 joyous stories per month, and 4,320 joyous stories per year. This must explain why I am so optimistic about life.

While listening to all these joyous moment stories, I have noticed one intriguing observation. When I ask the joyous moment question, some people do not show a happy face. I intentionally sound serious and ask the question seriously. Due to my Ethiopian English accent some English speaking people do not understand the question immediately. (Yes, this is true.)

Once they understand the question, I always see an involuntary smile on the face of the person. Then I start smiling and announce that, "I can see an involuntary smile and joy on your face," which makes them smile more and relax more to continue the conversation.

While some people, like Tom, can immediately think of their joyous moment and share the story, many others have a hard time thinking of their most joyous moment of the last 24 hours. I watch the person's face while searching for the joyous moment story. While their brain is searching for the joyous moment, without exception, there is this joyous facial expression.

- I have asked complete strangers to share their joyous moment of the last 24 hours.

- I have asked acquaintances to share their joyous moment of the day.

- I have asked clients to share their joyous moments.

- In group meetings, I have asked everyone to share their joyous moments of the last 24 hours.

In all these instances, I have always shared my joyous moment of the last 24 hours. When responding to the question about their joyous moment, everyone is sharing their personal story.

My brand of networking focuses on generating a positive story and a positive energy because networking is and must be a happy human interaction. Joy and happiness love company.

Who? Who are the key actors in networking?	Participants of networking include: everyone, you, and me. There are no spectators in networking.

Networking is like a two person or a group dance. Everyone on the dance floor participates. No spectators. I often find myself facilitating networking sessions as an active participant. My most common networking activity is with another person, where both of us equally participate.

My networking participants have been complete strangers or acquaintances or friends or family members. I have also facilitated networking activities with 3 or more people participating. Regardless of the number of people, everyone participates in the networking activity.

There are two major factors that drive participation by all actors. These are:

1) Creating a level field for all actors to participate; and

2) Role modeling by the networking session moderator to share deeper and more meaningful stories.

Creating a Level Field for all Actors to Participate.

This is an important ingredient to encourage everyone's participation. In asking any of my three favorite networking questions, I make sure everyone at the table shares their stories.

To ensure everyone participates:

- I gently remind the group that no one person dominates or does all the talking so that we do not miss out hearing from the less assertive people who may have an amazing and worthwhile story that is beneficial and inspiring.

- I discourage side conversations so that everyone benefits from the networking activity.

- I instruct the group that there is no right or wrong responses, and no one is allowed to judge, criticize, debate, or ridicule any of the inputs. This is designed to encourage less assertive participants by creating a safe group sharing environment.

Role Modeling by the Networking Session Moderator

Encourage sharing deeper and more meaningful stories.

My # 2 favorite question is:

"Who is one of your favorite family members and why?"

Some participants may be reluctant to put out their entire family story. To minimize this reluctance and encourage personal storytelling, I routinely share my own true story in response to this question about favorite family members.

Favorite Family Members Story #1

My dad, nicknamed *Tuka*, is one of my all-time favorite family members. He is a practicing, good Muslim man. He sent me to attend a Swedish Mission School. (Yes, he intentionally did it.) He sent my younger brother Beshir to the Koran School. He sent my two other younger brothers Tesfaye and Yacob to attend the Ethiopian Orthodox Church School. I admire my dad for showing us and for showing the world that he is as inclusive as it gets.

While I am a practicing Pentecostal Evangelical Christian, my dad remains my role model for religious tolerance. Consequently, I have no sympathy for people of faith who ridicule or belittle people of other faiths. When I meet people of any religion, I am least concerned about the doctrine of their faith.

The first thing I see is that they remind me of my family, and I see them as my brethren. I am sure this story tells you so much about me and the DNA of my value system. This story is bound to resonate with and attract certain kinds of people into my orbit. This is precisely the purpose behind networking based on storytelling.

Favorite Family Members Story #2

Two of my other favorite family members are my brother Teneshu and Uncle Korso.

When I was growing up, one of my favorite pastimes was to watch my people, the Arsi villagers, who often congregated under some big trees for shade to deliberate over day to day communal matters.

As a young child, I have to admit, I was mostly bored by the discussions and by most of the stories. However, there were times when I paid attention and when I thoroughly enjoyed the stories. Teneshu and Korso were the youngest of all the village elders. Despite their youth and inexperience, they commanded the respect of the village elders.

When they spoke everyone listened, paid attention, and laughed. Why? Teneshu and Korso always demonstrated wisdom and humor. I always saw smiles on their faces when they spoke. Their remarks were always memorable. Watching the genius of Teneshu and Korso has inspired me to try to make sure my public remarks and presentations are always memorable, impart some elements of wisdom and insight, and are laced with humor.

Why	Networking matters because it creates
Why does networking matter?	human connections, it allows learning about others, and it helps us learn about ourselves.

The primary and most important purpose of networking is to make human connections. In networking, we learn about others at a deeper level. We learn about ourselves.

At my family dinner table and when we drive, we share individual joyous moments of the day. We never run out of stories to share every day. In the process, we make deeper connections with one another and continue to gain better understanding of what each of us value in life. When we have guests for dinner or when we ride together, we follow the same process and our guests enjoy entering our circle of connection.

As a habitual networker, I come across three groups of people:

Category 1– people who have career advancement ambitions, including job seekers and those who seek promotional opportunities.

Category 2 – people who are entrepreneur types, including those in the startup stage and those with established businesses.

Category 3 – stakeholders who are prospects and clients who are likely to sponsor one of my business or philanthropic initiatives. In networking in these two circles, here is a summary of some examples of values realized:

(1) I recently met with Karla Indira Silvestre, Director of Community Engagement at Montgomery College. Karla's direct report, Hamrawit Tesfa, arranged the meeting to explore collaboration between Montgomery College and Go Pro21 Community. Within the first 5 minutes of our conversation, Karla and discovered that we are both alums of Florida State University and that Karla's husband is from Jacksonville, FL, as am I. BAM! Our human connection was made within minutes of meeting, which made our business meeting much smoother.

(2) A few years ago, Amy Foster, a good friend of mine, had a book release event hosted by a mutual friend, Sammy. I discovered something very profound that night at that book release event. Of all the remarks made that evening, one of Amy's remarks helped me discover something about myself. Amy shared a family story of her dad asking every one of her siblings what they wanted to do when they grew up. Amy concluded that every one of her siblings, including herself, became what they declared

they wanted to be. Incidentally, Amy told her dad she wanted to be an author, and now she is on her third book. That story hit me like a bolt. The next day, I started writing the first edition of *You Become What You Say*, which was completed in one month. This is a story of how a book release event and the ensuing networking event hosted by my friend Sammy and starred by my friend Amy, helped me discover the author in me that I never knew existed.

(3) I first met Calvin when he visited my church, and he promptly pulled out his card and gave it to me. Before I even read the card, I was certain he is an entrepreneur. How did I know? It takes one to know one. I am an entrepreneur, and I do not remember a day I have gone anywhere without my business cards. As Calvin and I continued to network, I learned that he is six sigma certified. At the time, my firm, ICATT Consulting, had a six sigma client training program scheduled. A week before the scheduled time, the trainer had to pull out for health reasons. I immediately called Calvin and he agreed to teach the class. This is an example of how networking can be a great tool to discover a person's capabilities that can be useful later on. Both Calvin and I continue to collaborate in our businesses and we both volunteer at Go Pro21 Community.

When When is networking most appropriate?	Networking is most appropriate when we first meet and greet, during the first part of an important meeting, and in a meeting dedicated to learning about and practicing networking.

There are three instances when networking is conducted:

1) When meeting and greeting for the very first time – networking is an excellent informal way to know a person we are working with.

2) In the first part of a working meeting – networking creates a conducive environment to engage in serious work.

3) In a meeting dedicated to networking – sessions dedicated to networking provide an excellent opportunity to learn networking skills and provide an expanded opportunity to learn about the participants.

In standing conference call meetings with my colleagues, I often gently ask that we start our meetings by sharing our joyous moments since our last meeting. I often explain that we share joyous moments so that we do not treat one another like robots who are only dedicated to working and do not have a need to connect; but, as humans we have a constant need for making connections with one another. Consequently, we continue to make connections with colleagues and carry each other's burdens in times of need.

What are clues that you may want to detour from a technical discussion to a networking lane?

- You are having a serious conversation with a person and you do not even know the name of the person. It is time to stop the conversation and engage in a networking activity.

- You are in a no win and heated debate for which there is no known reward for the winner of the debate. It is time to stop the debate and get in a networking activity.

- You are getting ready to engage in a working session with people you do not know very well. It is advisable to start the meeting with a get to know you networking activity.

- You are getting ready to engage in a serious working session with colleagues. Yes, you may know more about your regular colleagues, but you do not know their frame of mind now. Do you know if they won the lotto the night before? Do you know if they are not feeling well or a family member is ill? There may be some event in their life that affects the process and outcome of the meeting.

How? How is networking best implemented?	Networking is best implemented through personal storytelling, active listening, reciprocation, and keen observation.

For effective networking, participants must have the following skills:

1) *Personal storytelling* – ability to tell relevant stories about themselves.

2) *Active listening* – ability to ask questions to accurately comprehend the message conveyed by the speaker.

3) *Reciprocation* – ability to complement and follow instructions of the networking activity.

4) *Observation* – ability to sense the verbal as well as the non-verbal messages that are transmitted.

Two Conditions for the Networking Model to Work

For networking to have the intended outcomes, two conditions must be met:

1) *Willingness of participants* – the participants must be willing to learn and follow the networking instructions. This means the participants must believe in the value of networking.

2) *Capable moderator* – a networking activity is as good as the moderator who is conducting the session. A capable moderator can set the tone, explain the process, and serve as a role model by answering the questions that participants are asked to answer. More importantly, the moderator must believe in the value of the networking activities she is moderating.

Written & Group Networking Activity

1. *What is your joyous moment of the last 24 hours? (This may be a personal joyous moment or a business joyous moment.)*

2. *What is the history behind your name? (Meaning? Who gave you the name? Why were you given this name?)*

3. *Who is one of your favorite family members? Why?*

What are the general benefits of networking?

- <u>Forming strategic partnerships</u>: Two small businesses with complementary capabilities may form a mutually beneficial strategic partnership. For example, a home renovation expert and an online distributor of home renovation supplies may decide to form an alliance.

- <u>Gaining access to expertise</u>: You can gain access to a wide range of inputs, expertise, and experience.

- <u>Testing viability of ideas</u>: Networking gives you the opportunity to test ideas you want to implement.

- <u>Sharing knowledge</u>: Networking is a great avenue for sharing knowledge, insights, and best practices.

- <u>Creating opportunities</u>: Your next job or contract opportunity may present itself at a networking event or through informal networking.

- <u>Expanding contacts</u>: The people you meet at networking events can connect you with others when they see a match between you and their contacts.

- <u>Increasing visibility</u>: As you continue to network, you increase your visibility. This means you will come to mind when someone needs your services or comes across an opportunity you seek.

Written Activity

Which of the listed benefits have you realized from your networking experience?

List additional benefits (not listed above) you have realized from your networking experience?

Do you want networking to be your second nature? Try practicing these networking actions:

1. <u>When you are around people, unplug from electronic communication devices and tune in to the people around you.</u> Give full attention to the people around you by being totally focused and in the moment. How: monitor your electronic devices during a pre-scheduled time; place devices on mute or vibrate mode during important conversations; focus your attention on one important activity at a time; excuse yourself to attend to pressing matters rather than multi-tasking.

2. <u>At events, sit next to complete strangers.</u> Sitting with strangers at events allows you to meet new contacts and make new friends.

3. <u>When you meet people, convey friendliness with a generous smile.</u> You look good when you smile. You feel good when you smile. A smiling face attracts people.

4. <u>Repeat and learn a name.</u> Addressing a person by their name is like music to their ears. Remembering the names of people is a great networking habit. One way to remember a name is to repeatedly use the name during the first meeting.

5. <u>Bring some element of excitement to a conversation.</u> People tend to be attentive and engaged when there is excitement and positive energy in a conversation. How: share fun facts; use a sense of humor; share relevant success stories; refrain from complaining and bad mouthing others.

6. <u>Highlight what you have in common.</u> De-emphasis your differences. Try to identify and point out what you have in common. While dwelling on your differences drives you apart, your common interests draws you together.

7. <u>Maintain positive conversation.</u> A positive conversation is intentionally choosing positive words and positive stories that are inspiring and uplifting. A positive conversation contributes to maintaining a pleasant and healthy relationship.

8. <u>Seize a natural opportunity to enter into a conversation.</u> Conversations around you may be of interest and provide an opening for you to join in. How: listen to conversations around you; pay attention to people around you; intervene with a relevant question or remark.

9. Be curious to learn about people you meet. People generally enjoy telling their insightful and good stories. Your curiosity about the special talents of others allows people to tell their stories. This will increase your learning and enrichment.

10. Continue to grow your circle of people through ongoing engagement and networking. One of the clear indicators of your successful power networking is the growing number of acquaintances you are able to convert into your circle of networking hub. Here are some actions for nurturing your relationship with people you meet: invite them to attend events of common interest; send items of interest that benefit them; introduce them to contacts they may wish to meet; follow up on the status of any commitments you made the last time you were in contact with them; break bread with them.

11. Multiply the effects of your networking by recycling insights and success stories you gain from networking events. When you hear inspiring and exciting stories in one networking event, repeat them in other networking events. How: ensure relevance to the conversation, prior to recycling success stories; refer to people you have met in other networking events; acknowledge success stories of people from other networking events; ask for permission before you give out contact information of other people.

12. Early in a conversation, ask strategic questions to identify common areas of interest. If two people are having an engaging conversation, it is very likely they are discussing something they have in common. Here are some proven strategic questions that may uncover a common area of interest: What is your most exciting accomplishment of the day? Where are you from?

13. Offer assistance when asked and when appropriate. Your networking buddy may be new to town and looking for a good family restaurant. It is helpful to the other party when your recommendation of a restaurant is based on your positive experience and the experiences of others. Resist the slippery slope of offering general advice to strangers without knowing their full story.

14. Remember to strategically brag about your accomplishments. Strategic bragging is selectively telling a relevant and light story that puts you in a positive light.

15. Ask for suggestions about your desired career goal. If you are looking for a new job or seeking a promotional opportunity, it is a good idea to ask an open ended question seeking insight on how to go about reaching your career goal.

Resist the temptation to directly ask the person to hire you or to help you find a job. Such direct demands put undue pressure on the person.

16. <u>Restate follow up action items.</u> In the course of your networking conversation you may have agreed to reconnect for coffee next week. At the end of your talk, you will restate that you will get together for coffee next week. Better yet, place your appointment on your electronic calendars right away.

17. <u>Offer helpful insights that your new acquaintance finds beneficial</u>. Once you understand the expressed interests and needs of a person, you are in a better position to add value by offering relevant insights. How: actively listen to what they express; if you are not certain of their interests or needs, ask clarifying questions; use "I" statements when offering helpful insights. (Example: "If you are interested, I will be delighted to introduce you to two hiring managers, who happen to be my friends.")

18. <u>Seek insights and actions that you will implement to benefit you</u>. Remember, networking is a two-way street. If you find insights or resources you are able to use, feel free to do so. How: ask for permission before implementing their insights or resources; ask follow up questions for more insights and resources; generously express gratitude for value you have gained.

19. <u>Increase your knowledge about your new acquaintances</u>. By knowing a little more about the person's interests, background, expertise, and desired goals, you may add value for them and/or draw value from the conversation. How: ask open ended questions (examples: What is your claim to fame? What are you looking for?); follow up open ended questions with close ended question for clarity and confirmation (examples: How long have you been in this profession? How soon are you looking for a new job?); positively reinforce when you learn a piece of information (example: upon learning the person served in the military, thank them for their service).

20. <u>Ask "why" questions when you hear people expressing views you do not agree with</u>. As human beings, we have similarities and differences of opinion. While our similarities tend to pull us together, our differences may sometimes lead to conflicts and could lead to premature severance of good relationships. How: ask the first "why" question to learn the surface reason behind a person's view; ask subsequent "why" questions to give you deeper reasons that drive a person's belief; ensure your tone is positive and genuinely inquiring rather than judgmental.

21. <u>Seek to maintain balance between what you share and what you gain from your conversation partner</u>. Successful power networking allows both parties comparable time to talk. If you find yourself doing most of the talking, allow the other person to share by asking open ended questions. If you find the other person consuming most of the time, engage in active listening. You may want to put a time limit on the conversation. For example, you may say, "I need to be in the next meeting in 10 minutes."

22. <u>End networking conversations on a pleasant note.</u> Find a creative way to leave the person on an uplifting and pleasant note. This may include any of the following actions: let them know you enjoyed talking to them and look forward to future conversations; give them a high five, as appropriate; a hug, as appropriate; or just give them a big smile.

What if you are an introvert?

Networking may come very naturally to extroverts. Extroverts are people who are energized by talking and connecting with other people. Introverts are people who prefer to process information that comes their way through reflection in solitude. While extroverts are energized by contact with others, it takes introverts more energy to connect. Here are tips for introverts to successfully network:

- Start with your comfort area. At a networking venue, start networking with people you already know or with people who are introverts like yourself.

- Here are some open ended questions that can get you started: What is your favorite part of the day and why? What aspect of your work do you enjoy the most? Who is your favorite co-worker and why?

- You may focus on spending time with just a few people you meet; there is no need to compete with the extroverts who have met everyone in the room.

- Feel free to find someone who tells long stories and listen to their stories and ask probing questions. Remember, listening is the most endearing networking skill.

Developing the Four Networking Muscles

The four networking muscles include:

Networking Muscle #1: Friendly Greetings

Networking Muscle #2: Presenting Your Elevator Speech

Networking Muscle #3: Playing Networking Bingo

Networking Muscle #4: Speed Networking

Networking Muscle #1: Developing the Habit of Friendly Greetings

All networking begins with a good friendly greeting.

What are friendly greetings?

Friendly greetings means expressing a welcoming and friendly verbal and nonverbal message to people you meet every day. These expressions include:

- maintaining eye contact
- smiling, asking how they are doing
- introducing yourself
- shaking hands
- making small talk
- and related friendly gestures.

What methods of friendly greetings are most comfortable for you?

Why practice friendly greetings?

Here are the benefits of friendly greetings:

- You make a positive first impression on people you meet

- You look good

- You feel good

- It contributes to your good health

- It enhances your professional outcomes

What other benefits of friendly greetings can you think of?

Here are the benefits of friendly greetings to the recipients:

- They feel welcome

- It helps alleviate emotional issues

- They receive encouragement

- It makes a human connection

- It gives a feeling of belonging

What other benefits of friendly greetings to recipients can you think of?

Here are the benefits of friendly greetings to the mission or organization where this is practiced:

- In theory, people affiliate themselves with an organization because of their alignment with the mission. In practice, people truly maintain affiliation with an organization based on their positive experience there.

- An organization is its people. When people like an organization, it is because of the people they are connected with. When people leave an organization, it is often due to the people.

- Helps attract members.

- Helps retain members.

- People want to be more engaged with a friendly organization.

What are other benefits of friendly greetings to affiliate organizations?

Scientific Research Basis

A firm, friendly handshake has long been recommended in the business world as a way to make a good first impression, and the greeting is thought to date to ancient times as a way of showing a stranger you had no weapons.

New neuroscience research is confirming the old adage about the power of a handshake: strangers do form a better impression of those who offer their hand in greeting.

In a study conducted by psychologist Paula Niedenthal and colleagues at the University of Wisconsin, Madison, countries with greater immigration over the past 500 years were more likely to interpret smiles as friendly gestures.

Thus, if you come from a country of immigrants, you're more likely to crack a friendly smile on the street. That's the conclusion of this study, which may explain why Americans beam more than their Chinese and Russian counterparts.

How do you practice friendly greetings?

Let's take the steps of friendly greetings in slow motion:

Step One: Express Friendly Gesture

- Eye contact, smile, and words of greeting

Step Two: Engage in Small Talk

With a handshake, introduce yourself by your full name. Then learn light and fun stuff about the person.

Engage in discovering light items about the person as appropriate:

- *"Where are you from?"*

- *"What school did you attend?"*

You know these are easy and light items that people are delighted to share. Stay away from asking sensitive and controversial questions, such as:

- "Are you republican or democrat?"

- "What is your faith?"

- "What is your family status?"

Step Three: Share a Little bit About Yourself

Reciprocate and share light things about yourself such as…

- "I am a regular member here"

- "I am from…"

- "I am fan of …team"

- "I attended … school"

Step Four: Explore What You Have in Common

If time and situation permits, talk about items you have in common. You may be from same state or from neighboring states; you may have attended the same school; you may be fans of the same team. Something you have in common will make an easy, light conversation.

As part of this step, you may identify expressed needs for which you may know of helpful resources. For example, you may know of resources in response to employment needs or health needs they may have expressed. You may offer insights and contacts to help with expressed needs.

Step Five: Follow Up Actions

Follow up actions include:

- Exchanging contact information

- Agreeing to reconnect

- Invitations to events of interest

- Praying for each other

Explain best practices you have used in exchanging friendly greetings.

Practice Activity

1. *Give eye contact, smile, and say "how are you doing today" to as many people as you meet this week anywhere you go.*

2. *Try to keep a count of how many people you meet and greet the entire week.*

   (a) An estimate of how many people you managed to greet in this manner

   (b) How did you feel as you greeted different people in this manner?

   (c) What were some of the reactions from the people you greeted?

Networking Muscle #2: Developing and Delivering Your Elevator Speech Makes a Good First Impression

What is an elevator speech?

An elevator speech, also known as an elevator pitch is a brief, clear 'commercial' about you. It communicates about your professional personality, your present employment status, future job avenues you are looking for, and unique qualities you possess that can benefit an organization or a company. It is typically between 30 to 120 seconds in length – the time it takes people to ride from the top to the bottom of a building in an elevator.

Prepare your self-introduction/elevator speech here:

My name is _____

My claim to fame (what I am known for) is:

_____

The type of food or drink that best describes me is _____

Because _____

My current position is _____

My career aspiration is _____

My joyous moment of the day is

_____

My immediate need is _____

Your elevator speech presentation guidelines

- You entire elevator speech must be done in 1 minute.

- Be very loud for everyone in the room to hear you.

- Smile when you talk.

- Add a little humor.

- Be memorable.

Networking Muscle #3: Networking Bingo

Networking bingo is a structured networking exercise that allows you to learn one fact about a person and to further discuss that one fact. Networking bingo is used when you have a group meeting and you want to the attendees to meet and greet each other in a structured way. Some people are good networkers and others are not. Networking bingo is a great equalizer and allows all attendees to have a good reason to mix and mingle.

Networking bingo allows you to connect with people by discovering their unique attributes. When you approach a person, ask if they have experience in one of the boxes. If so, have them initial the box. Offer your experience to fill out one of the boxes. Engage in follow up conversation on the item checked. Limit one person for each item only to meet as many people as possible. If you meet 16 people to match your boxes, you are a true master networker.

Networking Bingo Ground Rules

- An item in one box only matches one person.

- After matching a person to an item in a box, this activity is intended to help you get to know a person.

- The game winner is the person who is able to match as many items in the box with the people in the room.

Networking Bingo Steps

1. When you receive a bingo sheet, write down your name at the top of the page.

2. After extending a friendly greeting, match a person with an item in one box. Limit one person to one item only. Take turns to complete one box per person and obtain an initial from one another.

3. After completing each box per person, have a brief and two way conversation regarding a matched item.

4. Repeat the process with as many people as possible.

5. When you are done, submit your sheet to the moderator to determine the top winners and prize recipients.

Sample Networking Bingo Sheet:

Is first born in my family	Has a pet	Lives near a family member	Is left handed
Speaks multiple languages	Has more than 5 brothers or sisters	Has flown out of country in the last 6 months	Plays a musical instrument
Moved a great distance recently	Plays a sports game	Has a close friend born outside the U.S.	Has been promoted twice in the last year
Likes pizza	Volunteers	Conducted a public presentation in the last 6 months	Vacationed overseas at least twice.

Networking Muscle #4: Speed Networking Ground Rules

Speed networking is spending a max of 10 minutes of conversation exchange with each person you meet.

Please take turns to ask/answer these questions:

1) My name is (give full name) with a gently firm handshake and a contagious friendly smile.

2) What is your joyous moment of your entire week or the last 24 hours? Have a conversation on this exchange.

3) What are your special gifts/talents/strengths? Make sure you ask more probing questions to learn specifics.

4) What is your expertise/professional background? Make sure you ask more probing questions to learn specifics.

5) What are you trying to accomplish in this networking event?

In conclusion, you briefly agree on any follow up items and pleasantly part ways and move on to the next networking partners.

Concluding remarks

Networking is making friends at your every interaction with others. Networking is strengthening your existing relationships and making new positive relationships.

The networking framework answers five basic questions: *What? Who? Why? When? How?*

- *What* is the principal content of networking? The principal content of networking is a personal story including: everyone's stories, your story, and my story.

- *Who* are the key actors in networking? Participants of networking include: everyone, you, and me. There are no spectators in networking.

- *Why* does networking matter? Networking creates human connections; it allows learning about others; it helps us learn about ourselves.

- *When* is networking most appropriate? Networking is most appropriate: when we first meet and greet; during the first part of an important meeting; and in a meeting dedicated to learning about and practicing networking.

- *How* is networking best implemented? Networking is best implemented through: personal storytelling, active listening; reciprocation; and keen observation.

General benefits of networking include:

- Forming strategic partnerships

- Gaining access to expertise

- Testing the viability of ideas

- Sharing knowledge

- Creating opportunities

- Increasing visibility.

Some strategies of networking are:

- When you are around people, unplug from electronic communication devices and tune in to the people around you.

- At events, sit next to complete strangers.

- When you meet people, convey friendliness with a generous smile, Also, repeat and learn their names.

- Highlight what you have in common, be curious to learn about people you meet, and remember to strategically brag about your accomplishments.

- Ask *why* questions when you hear people expressing views you do not agree with.

There are four networking muscles that you can develop to help you become a pro at networking:

1) Develop the habit of friendly greetings.

2) Prepare and practice presenting your elevator speech to convey a consistent message about yourself.

3) Regularly play networking bingo as practice for naturally learning personal attributes of people you meet.

4) Actively participate in speed networking to help you expand your circle of contacts.

Networking is the most powerful interpersonal skills you can use to accomplish your personal interest goals as well as your community interest goals. The more you learn and practice networking, the more effective you become and the more it works for you.

End of Chapter Activity

1. *What is the state of your networking practice?*

2. *Prepare and present your elevator speech.*

3. *What deliberate actions are you ready to implement your take your networking to the next level?*

The currency of real networking is not greed but generosity.

— Keith Ferrazzi

Chapter 7

Coopetition-Oriented Teamwork
How Collaborating With Your Rivals Creates a Win-Win

Selected Quotes

If You Can't Beat 'Em, Work with 'Em

— The Amazon Model

A flower does not think of competing with the flower next to it. It just blooms.

— Zen Chin

Two are better off than one, because together they can work more effectively. If one of them falls down, the other can help him up.

— Ecclesiastes 4:9-12

As iron sharpens iron, so one person sharpens another.

— Proverbs 27:17

Talent wins games, but teamwork and intelligence wins championships.

— Michael Jordan

On our own, we are marshmallows and dried spaghetti, but together we can become something bigger.

— C.B. Cook

We = power
— Lorii Myers, Targeting Success, Develop the Right Business Attitude to be Successful in the Workplace

If two men on the same job agree all the time, then one is useless. If they disagree all the time, both are useless.

— Darryl F. Zanuck

Abstract

Coopetition-oriented teamwork is collaboration among competing and convergent group of people in order to achieve a common interest, mutual benefits, or higher purpose. Members of the team may be competitors or may have divergent beliefs, backgrounds, ethnicity, skills, interests, politics, nationality, personalities, values, and any combination of attributes.

The anatomy of coopetition-oriented teamwork answers five basic questions: *What? Who? Why? When? How?*

- *What* is coopetition-oriented teamwork? Collaboration among a competing and divergent group of people in order to achieve a common and complex interest.

- *Who* are members of coopetition-oriented teams? Members have divergent attributes such as nationality, religion, religious denominations, ethnicity, professional background, political philosophy, personality style, and other human attributes. They may also be competitors.

- *Why* does coopetition-oriented teamwork matter? Divergent attributes are the breeding ground for innovation and creativity.

- *When* is coopetition-oriented teamwork appropriate? Coopetition-oriented teamwork is most appropriate when the desired common interest is too important and too complex for individual effort or the work of a homogenous team.

- *How* does coopetition-oriented teamwork work? It works by providing good leadership, using deep diversity for team formation, using knowledge sharing, and using emotional intelligence.

General benefits of teamwork include:

- Potential for achieving extraordinary outcomes

- Improved morale, increased creativity, and innovation

- Fosters continuous learning

- Builds trust

- Teaches conflict resolution skills

- Encourages healthy risk taking.

General teamwork strategies include:

- Open mindedness

- Open communication

- Maintain interpersonal relations

- Empower team members

- Support mission

- Encourage complementary strengths

- Foster mutual respect

- Adopt a common approach.

Coopetition-oriented teamwork is a force multiplier that can take individual efforts to new heights of accomplishment. With constant alignment of team members with the common interest and with cultivated synergies among team members, the journey and the destination of coopetition-oriented teams can be extraordinary.

Rate Your Current level of Coopetition-Oriented Teamwork
(1=Poor, 2=Below Average, 3=Average, 4=Good, 5=Excellent)

Coopetition-Oriented Teamwork Actions	1=Poor 5=Excellent (circle one)
1. You successfully work with team members who possess very divergent attributes such as nationality, gender, religion, ethnicity, and professional backgrounds.	1 2 3 4 5
2. You have a positive experience in successfully accomplishing very complex and and very important interests of importance to society.	1 2 3 4 5
3. You are good at finding a common ground with your rivals.	1 2 3 4 5
4. You maintain positive and constructive communication with your frenemies.	1 2 3 4 5
5. You maintain supportive and encouraging interpersonal relationships with all stakeholders.	1 2 3 4 5
6. You empower team members to make decisions and be accountable for their actions.	1 2 3 4 5
7. You are aligned with and believe in the mission of the team.	1 2 3 4 5
8. You encourage team members with complementary skills.	1 2 3 4 5
9. You foster a culture of mutual respect for all stakeholders regardless of a person's role.	1 2 3 4 5
10. You adopt a common approach based on inputs from stakeholders with differing strengths.	1 2 3 4 5

Your total score is _____

Assess your score:

40 +	Outstanding
30 +	Very Good
25 +	Good
Below 25	Needs Improvement

Coopetition-Oriented Teamwork Success Story

Note: The purpose of this story is to illustrate the application of principles and skills covered in this chapter. The story is based on character elements of real people I know personally, but the details and events are my creative work designed for illustrative purposes.

Catherine, Charles, and Gabe each own their respective businesses and are Business to Business (B2B) partners. Thus, they are competitors. The trio collaborated to win and implement a federal training contract.

Catherine is gifted in asking questions to sort out wishful thinking from real opportunities. She is adept at listening for a total message from the client. So, she is very good at reading the client. Her role in the B2B collaboration is to manage client relations.

Charles is very good at consensus building among team members. He focuses on the big prize and resists the temptation to get sucked into petty stuff. He possesses the intangibles of a trusted teaming partner. He wins trusted friends with his empathy-savvy. His role in the teaming partnership became contract manager.

Gabe is a possibility thinker. He is incredibly resourceful and creates viable solutions for challenging situations. He is often ready to act on the course of action the group wants to accomplish. Gabe became the operations manager.

The B2B teaming partners leaned on their individual as well as collective strengths to achieve an extraordinary accomplishment. The path of their collaborative effort was far from a walk in the park. There were challenges along the way. There were occasional disagreements, conflicting expectations, miscommunications, and misunderstanding of motives. With patience and wisdom, they prevailed over these natural teaming challenges. Long after this initial partnership, they readily call on one another for networking, seeking each other's advice, and collaboration.

Success Story Discussion Questions

What is a common interest that brought these competitors together? Explain.

What is your solution to address a major teamwork challenge that the B2B are likely to encounter?

Definition of Coopetition-Oriented Teamwork

Coopetition-oriented teamwork is collaboration among competing and convergent groups and people in order to achieve a common interest and a bigger purpose.

Team members may be rivals and may have divergent beliefs, backgrounds, ethnicity, skills, interests, politics, nationality, personalities, values, and any combination of attributes. What brings together a coopetition-oriented team is a common and complex interest that is important for all team members.

Introducing the Business Roots of Coopetition

Coopetition is a business strategy that uses insights gained from game theory to understand when it is better for competitors to work together.

Coopetition games are mathematical models that are used to examine in what ways cooperation among competitors can increase the benefits to all players and grow the market. The models also examine when it's best to allow competition to divide the existing benefits among players in order to provide the leading competitors with more market share.

The coopetition model starts out with a diagramming process called the value net, which is represented as a diamond with four defined player designations at the corners. The players are customers, suppliers, competitors and complementors (competitors whose products add value). The goal of coopetition is to move the players from a zero-sum game, in which the winner takes all and the loser is left empty-handed, to a plus-sum game, a scenario in which the end result is more profitable when the competitors work together. An important part of the game is to learn which variables will influence the players to either compete or cooperate and when it is to a player's advantage not to cooperate.

Coopetition (also spelled co-opetition) is a portmanteau, combining the words cooperation and competition. The principles and practices of coopetition are credited to Harvard and Yale business professors, Adam M. Brandenburger and Barry J. Nalebuff. Competitive businesses that also cooperate when it is to their advantage are said to be in coopetition.

The Amazon Model: *If You Can't Beat 'Em, Work with 'Em*

In *Strategy + Business*'s June 2, 2014 publication, Matt Palmquist chronicles various business cases, examples and benefits of the Amazon model of "If You Can't Beat 'Em, Work with 'Em."

Amazon is a pioneer in applying coopetition. In late 2000, Amazon introduced the "Amazon Marketplace," which enabled competitors of any size to use Amazon's online platform and technological capabilities to present their millions of new, used, and rare books to millions of customers. By the second quarter of 2002, Amazon reported that third-party transactions represented 20 percent of its North American sales, and by 2010, the marketplace accounted for more than 35 percent of sales. Coopetition remains the centerpiece of Amazon's unconventional growth strategy.

Allowing Rivals Wins

One lesson that other businesses can learn from the Amazon approach is to let the competitor win by inviting rivals into its business model and thus creating a larger overall market. By doing this, a firm can potentially capture a bigger share for itself down the road. For example, in the AIM alliance between Apple, IBM, and Motorola, fierce competitors in the personal computer market co-created new microprocessors, which enabled them to open new markets and opportunities for all parties.

Efficient Use of Resources.

The second takeaway: firms can use their resources more efficiently when they share or leverage them with competitors through a coopetition-based setup. A coopetition relationship between Sony and Samsung enabled the two direct competitors to establish joint technology and manufacturing plants in South Korea that has helped them become market leaders in the LCD TV segment over the past decade. The two companies leveraged Sony's technological knowledge and Samsung's marketing abilities to expand the global LCD TV market and make the two companies dominant in their fields.

Many forms of coopetition.

Coopetition may be used for sharing of costs, distribution channels, innovation efforts, marketing campaigns, and risks.

Introducing 'Frenemy' as a Related Concept of Coopetition

According to mydictionary.com, a 'frenemy' is someone who is both a friend and an enemy. An example of a 'frenemy' is someone who you are nice to in person, but secretly compete with.

According to Urban Dictionary, Winston Churchill is credited with first coining this term while discussing America's involvement in WW2. "America is Britain's first and only 'Frenemy.' It is this country which will help with one hand while competing with another hand."

A 'frenemy' is a person or group that is friendly toward another because the relationship brings benefits, but harbors feelings of resentment or rivalry. Clearly, turning the competition into 'frenemies' can be beneficial to achieve mutual organizational or personal goals. For example, there seems to be a 'frenemy' relationship between Google and other search engines.

In an article titled: <u>Frenemies with Benefits</u>, Matt Palmquit concludes that, "When their profit goals differ, fiercely competitive firms may decide to collaborate with each other on complementary offerings."

According to Palmquist, traditionally, companies vying for dominance of their industry have viewed the competition with a winner-takes-all mentality, striving to push their rivals out of the marketplace by attracting consumers exclusively to their own products or services. But the recent rise of multi-sided platforms — which allow consumers to use or buy goods and services from several complementary but competing firms – has changed the game.

For example, operating systems like Mac OS, Linux, and Windows connect consumers with third-party software firms that develop applications and, in turn, improve the central platform. In industries as diverse as media, retail, social networking, smartphones, and even credit cards, collaborating or partnering with complementary firms can make the focal offering more appealing to consumers.

From Coopetition to Frenemy to Coopetition-Oriented Teamwork

In the previous section, we have seen how high profile business enterprises like Amazon, Apple, Microsoft, IBM, Sony, Samsung and others have been able to seize a much bigger market share by a smart application of the concept of coopetition and 'frenemy.' Small businesses, civic organizations, and individuals who wish to score breakthrough level of success can benefit from these concepts as well.

American corporations lead their global rivals in innovation, rewriting the business rules and achieving breakthrough results. Factors that have contributed to their success are their ability to re-create themselves and their willingness to implement best practices. Start ups, small businesses, civic organizations and individuals who wish to achieve breakthrough results must be willing to take the bold steps of reinventing themselves and applying available best practices just like their corporate counterparts.

Coopetition-oriented teamwork is one of the best practices presented here for the benefit of organizations and individuals who wish to achieve extraordinary success. Coopetition-oriented teamwork builds on lessons from its underlying concepts to empower organizations and individuals to achieve extraordinary outcomes.

The following section will present an overview of the anatomy of coopetition-oriented teamwork. The framework is intentionally a very simple model. Why? The simplicity of the model may motivate you to try it out. Once you have a taste of how the model works, I believe in your ability to take your success into a higher gear. I believe in your ability to develop a more complex model to achieve more advanced outcomes.

Overview of Anatomy of Coopetition-Oriented Teamwork

The anatomy of coopetition-oriented teamwork answers five basic questions: *What? Who? Why? When? How?*

What? What is coopetition-oriented teamwork?	Collaboration among a competing and divergent group of people in order to achieve a common and complex interest. Some examples of common interests include: child safety, regional economic development, job creation, business growth, human rights, civil rights, global warming, national interests, and other complex and important interests.
Who? Who are members of coopetition-oriented Teams?	Members have divergent attributes. Some examples of divergent attributes include: nationality, religion, ethnicity, professional background, political philosophy, personality style, and other human attributes.
Why Why coopetition-oriented teamwork?	Coopetition-oriented teamwork contributes to innovation and creativity. Divergent attributes are the breeding ground of innovation and creativity. Extensive research shows the link between group divergence and innovation.
When When is coopetition-oriented teamwork appropriate?	Coopetition-oriented teamwork is most appropriate when the desired common interest impacts a cross-section of society and is too important and too complex for individual effort or the work of a homogenous team. For example: Recent mass shootings have impacted a

	cross-section of our society. Any attempt to prevent such acts require coopetition-oriented teamwork.
How? How does coopetition-oriented teamwork work?	Coopetition-oriented teamwork works by implementing evidence based key teamwork strategies such as providing good leadership, using deep diversity for team formation, using knowledge sharing, and using emotional intelligence.

Some reading this in the United States may point fingers at the elephant in the room: the United States Congress. So let's address this temptation upfront – let's bring up the United States Congress.

As a U.S. citizen, I understand the sentiment that the U.S. Congress can benefit from applying best practices in coopetition-oriented teamwork, particularly when we witness members of Congress seldom seeing eye to eye with those of the opposing political party. At times, the height of partisan divide is painful and a cause for great concern for many of our citizens.

Yet, while I certainly encourage members of the U.S. Congress to publicly demonstrate the application of coopetition-oriented teamwork, I'm among those people who feel that the U.S. Congress is just fine. Yes, you read it right: the U.S. Congress is just fine. Why? For one, democracy is a messy form of government. Still, it is the best system of government, where everyone is protected by the law and everyone is under the law. Second, I would take the messy U.S. Congress over a parliament under a dictatorial regime, where the members of parliament are so orderly and so quiet in order not to offend the rulers.

My argument for why the U.S. Congress is just fine is based on my first hand and personal experience with Congress in my capacity as a citizen advocate for causes I believe in. I have witnessed that the U.S. Congress relies heavily on applying the principles of coopetition-oriented teamwork. Members of Congress find a common ground on the majority of bills they pass. I also understand the frustrations of our citizenry who only see partisan bickering over a small list of items, where members of congress are more competitors and rivals. While the disagreements are only part of the story, I know that there is a lot bipartisan collaboration and deal making. The U.S. Congress is probably one institution that best applies coopetition-oriented teamwork. For the 3rd edition of this book, I plan to conduct case studies at the U.S. Congress in the application of coopetition-oriented teamwork. Stay tuned.

Anatomy of Coopetition-Oriented Teamwork Explained

What?	Collaboration among a competing and divergent group of people in order to achieve a common and complex interest.
What is coopetition-oriented teamwork?	
	Some examples of common interests include: child safety, regional economic development, job creation, business growth, human rights, civil rights, global warming, national interests, and other complex and important interests.

Coopetition-oriented teamwork is a new kind of teamwork.

Coopetition-oriented teamwork is collaboration among a competing and divergent group of people in order to achieve an important and complex common interest.

We live in an increasingly complex world. Advances in technology, the Internet of things, transportation technologies, telecommunication technologies, social media, collaboration technologies are all changing our lives at a progressively faster rate. The new realities are creating new opportunities, challenges, and interests. We used to live in a more black or white, monolithic, ethnic based and nationalistic world. The brave new world is colorful, multi-layered, increasingly diverse, and increasingly inclusive, where we will simply have to live with people who think, believe, look, speak, and value differently. Despite the apparent differences, we have common interests for well-being, safety, quality of life, mutual respect, coexistence, safe environments, prosperity, and other important and complex human interests.

Coopetition-oriented teamwork is a framework of choice to function in an increasingly shared economy. Uber and Lyft are making it possible to share our private cars with complete strangers. AirBNB is allowing us to share our private homes with strangers.

Coopetition-oriented teamwork focuses on common interests and less on the identities and attributes of the members. Some common interests that qualify for coopetition-oriented teamwork include:

- Ensuring child safety is of interest to parents with varying attributes.

- Securing safe drinking water is of interest to all who consume water.

- Advancing economic development is of interest to residents of a region.

- Maintaining violence free cities is of interest to all who value life.

- Guaranteed respect for human rights is of interest to all freedom loving people.

- Sustaining a nuclear free world is of interest to all occupants of our planet.

Group Discussion Activity

The next time you are with people with at least 3 attributes that are different from you, have a conversation to identify 3-5 important and complex interests that are important to all parties.

Who? Who are members of coopetition-oriented teams?	Members have divergent attributes. Some examples of divergent attributes include: nationality, religion, ethnicity, professional background, political philosophy, personality style, and other human attributes.

Members of coopetition-oriented teams are members of our society who happened to possess divergent attributes.

People with diverse backgrounds who have a stake in a common interest must be part of the desired solution. For example, ensuring child safety in a neighborhood is of interest to:

- Parents whose backgrounds are American, Mexican, Canadian, Russian, Chinese, and all other nationalities.

- Parents who are white, black, brown, yellow and any other pigmentation.

- Parents who are Catholics, Muslims, Sikhs, Agnostics, Buddhists and those of other faith groups.

- Parents who are conservatives, progressives, independents, and those of other political affiliations.

- Parents who are of military, civilian, independent contractor, entrepreneur, or other professional backgrounds.

- Parents who are male, female, married, and single.

While the listed divergent attributes have long been causes for separation and disagreements among people, the brave new world we live in calls for human reconnection on the strength of our common interests. In other words, these differences become the exact reason why we need each other.

Group Discussion Activity
The next time you are with your colleagues, have a friendly conversation to identify 3-5 divergent attributes among you.

Why?	Coopetition-oriented teamwork contributes to innovation and creativity.
Why coopetition-oriented teamwork?	
	Divergent attributes are the breeding ground of innovation and creativity. Extensive research shows the link between group divergence and innovation.

Coopetition-oriented teamwork is the most important contributor to the success of complex and important interests. Why? Very important and complex interests require innovation and creativity. Divergent attributes are the breeding ground for innovation and creativity.

In a January 2016 edition of the official SHRM professional magazine, Novid Parsi penned an article titled *Workplace Diversity and Inclusion Gets Innovative: Yesterday's workforce won't lead you into tomorrow.* In this article, Parsi asserts that diversity is a performance driver. According to Parsi, diversity is not just about mirroring the country's demographics. It's also about innovation and performance. Companies that exhibit gender and ethnic diversity are respectively, 15 percent and 35 percent more likely to outperform those that don't. Parsi sites the research by global management consulting firm McKinsey & Co. to point out that organizations with more racial and gender diversity bring in more sales revenue, more customers, and higher profits. Also, companies in the top quartile of executive-board diversity had returns on equity that were 53 percent higher than those in the bottom quartile. Moreover, organizations with more female executives are more profitable, according to a 2016 analysis of more than 20,000 firms in 91 countries.

In a Boston Consulting Group (BCG) online publication of April 26, 2017, titled *The Mix that Matters: Innovation through Diversity*, Lorenzo, R., et. al., pose an important research question:

When companies undertake efforts to make their management teams more diverse by adding women and people from other countries, industries, and companies, does it pay off?

According to this study of 171 German, Swiss, and Austrian companies, there is a clear relationship between the diversity of companies' management teams and the revenues they get from innovative products and services. The following are the major findings:

- The positive relationship between management diversity and innovation is statistically significant, meaning that companies with higher levels of diversity get more revenue from new products and services.

- The innovation boost isn't limited to a single type of diversity. The presence of managers who are female or from other countries, industries, or companies can cause an increase in innovation.

- Management diversity seems to have a particularly positive effect on innovation at complex companies – those that have multiple product lines or that operate in multiple industry segments. Diversity's impact also increases with company size.

- To reach its potential, gender diversity needs to go beyond tokenism. In the study, innovation performance only increased significantly when the workforce included a nontrivial percentage of women (more than 20%) in management positions. Having a high percentage of female employees doesn't do anything for innovation, the study shows, if only a small number of women are managers.

- At companies with diverse management teams, openness to contributions from lower-level workers and an environment in which employees feel free to speak their minds are crucial in fostering innovation.

Similar findings come from the Stanford University Clayman Institute for Gender Research, *Gender News*, (March 24, 2017). In an article titled, *How Does Diversity Spur Innovation*, Kilanski, K. reports research findings that suggest organizations with more diversity have higher levels of innovation.

Using laboratory experiments, Katherine Phillips and Margaret Neale analyzed the connections between race and innovation. They found that racially homogeneous groups tend to fall into the trap of "groupthink," or a situation that occurs "when a group values harmony and coherence over accurate analysis and critical evaluation." The authors argue that being around others who are similar tricks us into thinking everyone else shares the same information and perspectives. Groupthink can lead individuals to ignore missing information or alternate explanations that force the development of creative solutions. Furthermore, the consequences of groupthink are that people are not inclined to contribute individual insights that veer from the group norm or the group's accepted thoughts. This is especially true of women and minorities, who already are often outsiders and are often underrepresented in many workplaces; to offer criticism risks the potential of being seen as not a team player.

However, as Phillips, Neale, and other researchers have found, when a group is more socially heterogeneous, people are more likely to contribute their unique perspectives and knowledge, leading to better decision-making. Not only are people more willing to share what they know when they are in heterogeneous settings, being confronted by difference also sparks individuals to adopt a more holistic and sympathetic approach to problem solving by priming them to place themselves in other people's' shoes. In other words, says Phillips, "diversity makes us smarter."

In an article titled, "How Diversity can Drive Innovation," in the December 2013 *Harvard Business Review*, Hewlett, S., et. al., reported that businesses with more diverse leaders were more likely to report that they increased their market share and captured new markets in the past year than businesses with less diverse workforces.

The *Harvard Business Review* research provides compelling evidence that diversity unlocks innovation and drives market growth – a finding that should intensify efforts to ensure that executive ranks both embody and embrace the power of differences.

In a post titled, "Diversity + Inclusion = Better Decision Making at Work," from *Forbes online*, Sept 21, 2017, contributor Erik Larson reports findings from recent research about inclusive decision making to understand how much improvement is possible.

The study analyzed approximately 600 business decisions made by 200 different business teams in a wide variety of companies over two years. The research shows a direct link between inclusive decision making and better business performance:

- Inclusive teams make better business decisions up to 87% of the time.

- Teams that follow an inclusive process make decisions 2X faster with 1/2 the meetings.

- Decisions made and executed by diverse teams delivered 60% better results.

The preceding and diverse research studies show that diversity of a group yield better performance, innovation, creativity, and market share.

When?	Coopetition-oriented teamwork is most appropriate when the desired common interest impacts a cross-section of society and is too important and too complex for individual effort or the work of a homogenous team.
When is coopetition-oriented teamwork appropriate?	For example: Recent mass shootings have impacted a cross-section of our society. Any attempt to prevent such acts require coopetition-oriented teamwork.

Establishing and maintaining a divergent group is not an easy task. Thus, activities and causes that are extremely important and complex must be targeted as candidates for coopetition-oriented teamwork.

In an article titled, "Does Diversity Actually Increase Creativity," in *Harvard Business Review*, June 28, 2017, Tomas Chamorro-Premuzic shows a difference between generating ideas and implementing ideas. While diverse team composition does seem to confer an advantage when it comes to generating a wider range of original and useful ideas, experimental studies suggest that such benefits disappear once the team is tasked with deciding which ideas to select and implement, presumably because diversity hinders consensus.

A meta-analysis of 108 studies and more than 10,000 teams indicated that the creativity gains produced by higher team diversity are disrupted by the inherent social conflict and decision-making deficits that less homogeneous teams create. It would therefore make sense for organizations to increase diversity in teams that are focused on exploration or idea generation, and use more-homogeneous teams to curate and implement those ideas.

This distinction mirrors the psychological competencies associated with the creative process: divergent thinking, openness to experience, and mind wandering are needed to produce a large number of original ideas, but unless they are followed by convergent thinking, expertise, and effective project management, those ideas will never become actual innovations.

For all the talk about the importance of creativity, the critical piece is really innovation. Most organizations have a surplus of creative ideas that are never implemented, and more diversity is not going to solve this problem.

How?	Coopetition-oriented teamwork works by implementing evidence based key teamwork strategies such as providing good leadership, using deep diversity for team formation, using knowledge sharing, and using emotional intelligence.
How does coopetition-oriented teamwork work?	

In *Strategies that Increase Effectiveness of Coopetition-Oriented Teamwork,* Tomas Chamorro-Premuzic offers three initial strategies to increase the effectiveness of diverse groups, including:

- providing good leadership

- using deep diversity

- knowledge sharing.

Let's explain each:

Good leadership

The conflicts arising from diversity can be mitigated if teams are effectively led.

Deep-level diversity

Most discussions about diversity focus on demographic variables (e.g., gender, age, and race). However, the most interesting and influential aspects of diversity are psychological (e.g., personality, values, and abilities), also known as deep-level diversity. Indeed, there are several advantages to focusing on deep-level variables as opposed to demographic factors.

First, whereas demographic variables perpetuate stereotypical and prejudiced characterizations, deep-level diversity focuses on the individual, allowing a much more granular understanding of human diversity. Regardless of whether you focus on bright- or dark-side personality characteristics, motives and values, or indeed creativity, group differences are trivial when compared with differences between individuals, even when the individuals are part of the same group.

Knowledge sharing

No matter how diverse the workforce is, and regardless of what type of diversity we examine, diversity will not enhance creativity unless there is a culture of sharing knowledge.

Team Members Treating One Another Nice

In 2012, Google created a venture known as Project Aristotle to discover the magic formula for a successful team. Google's extensive study and analysis led to a finding that good teamwork is being nice. The Aristotle Project took several years and included interviews with hundreds of employees as well as analysis of data about the people on more than 100 active teams at the company. Google's data-driven approach ended up highlighting that the best teams respect one another's emotions and are mindful that all members should contribute to the conversation equally. It has less to do with who is in a team, and more with how a team's members interact with one another. In the best teams, members listen to one another and show sensitivity to feelings and needs.

General Benefits of Coopetition-Oriented Teamwork

Coopetition-oriented teamwork falls under the general category of teamwork. Despite the fact that membership and circumstances of a coopetition-oriented team is markedly different from a simple and homogeneous team, once such teams start working together, their success greatly depends on working as a team. In this case, coopetition-oriented teams can reap all the benefits of a normal team with one exception – the benefits of coopetitive-oriented teamwork are more potent.

Important benefits of teamwork

Improved morale: Teamwork allows team members to have ownership of the entire work process, which improves morale. Also, working on a team gives employees a sense of belonging and pride.

Increased creativity and innovation: Brainstorming and free flow of ideas and solutions within a team can lead to creativity and innovation. This is good for the organization to which the team belongs, and also leads to a sense of fulfillment and monetary incentives for team members.

Fosters continuous learning: Teamwork maximizes knowledge sharing and learning new skills. As team members learn new skills their value and promotability increases.

Builds trust: Sustained teamwork and interdependence among team members fosters trust. Trust leads to more confidence and improved quality of life for team members.

Teaches conflict resolution skills: Conflict is inevitable in teams. The opportunity to work through conflicts helps team members acquire skills in conflict resolution, thus developing savvy people skills.

Encourages healthy risk-taking: The interdependence within a team encourages team members to take more calculated risks. Such calculated risks may lead to the most innovative and breakthrough solutions.

General teamwork strategies

Again, coopetition-oriented teamwork falls within the family of general teamwork. Thus, coopetition-oriented teams can benefit from general teamwork strategies.

Open communication: Establish open lines of communication among all stakeholders. Maintain a culture of positive and constructive communication.

Maintain interpersonal relations: Maintain supportive and encouraging interpersonal relationships among all stakeholders.

Empower team members: Empower team members to make decisions and be accountable for their actions. Incentivize team members to ask for forgiveness rather than to ask for permission.

Support of mission: Criteria for joining a team must be based on alignment and belief in the mission of the team. The same criteria must be used for advancements and separation.

Encourage complementary strengths: A good team consists of members and stakeholders with complementary skills and views of mission accomplishment. Encourage and train team members to learn to communicate their unique perspective in a constructive manner. Also, train stakeholders to welcome expressions and demonstrations of complementary strengths.

<u>Foster mutual respect</u>: Create and foster a culture of mutual respect for all stakeholders regardless of each person's role.

<u>Adopt common approach</u>: Adopt a homegrown, common approach based on inputs from the differing strengths of stakeholders. A common approach within a team allows efficiency and promotes cost savings for the team.

Concluding Remarks

Coopetition-oriented teamwork is collaboration among competing and convergent group of people in order to achieve a common interest, mutual benefits, or higher purpose. Members of the team may be competitors or may have divergent beliefs, backgrounds, ethnicity, skills, interests, politics, nationality, personalities, values, and any combination of attributes.

The anatomy of the coopetition-oriented teamwork answers five basic questions: *What? Who? Why? When? How?*

- *What* is Coopetition-Oriented Teamwork? Collaboration among a competing and divergent group of people in order to achieve a common and complex interest.

- *Who* are members of Coopetition-Oriented Teams? Members have divergent attributes such as nationality, religion, religious denominations, ethnicity, professional background, political philosophy, personality style, and other human attributes. They may also be competitors.

- *Why* does Coopetition-Oriented Teamwork matter? Divergent attributes are the breeding ground for innovation and creativity.

- *When* is Coopetition-Oriented Teamwork appropriate? Coopetition-Oriented Teamwork is most appropriate when the desired common interest is too important and too complex for individual effort or the work of a homogenous team.

- *How* does Coopetition-Oriented Teamwork work? It works by providing good leadership, using deep diversity for team formation, using knowledge sharing, and using emotional intelligence.

General benefits of teamwork include:

- Potential for achieving extraordinary outcomes

- Improved morale, increased creativity, and innovation

- Fosters continuous learning

- Builds trust

- Teaches conflict resolution skills

- Encourages healthy risk taking.

General teamwork strategies include:

- Open mindedness

- Open communication

- Maintain interpersonal relations

- Empower team members

- Support mission

- Encourage complementary strengths

- Foster mutual respect

- Adopt a common approach.

Coopetition-Oriented Teamwork is a force multiplier that can take individual efforts to new heights of accomplishment. With constant alignment of team members with the common interest and with cultivated synergies among team members, the journey and the destination of Coopetition-Oriented teams can be extraordinary.

End of Chapter Written Activity

1.   *Identify 2-3 topics that are of interest to a wildly divergent group of people.*

2.   *List the the attributes of people you will include as a project team.*

3.   *What are your 3-5 anticipated challenges and your strategies to prevent these challenges.*

4.   *Share your personal experience with a frenemy.*

5.   *Share your personal experience with coopetition.*

References

6 Different Team Effectiveness Models to Understand Your Team Better
https://www.wrike.com/blog/6-different-team-effectiveness-models/

After years of intensive analysis, Google found the key to good teamwork is being nice:
https://work.qz.com/625870/after-years-of-intensive-analysis-google-discovers-the-key-to-good-teamwork-is-being-nice/

The Amazon Model: If You Can't Beat 'Em, Work with 'Em
https://www.strategy-business.com/blog/The-Amazon-Model-If-You-Cant-Beat-Em-Work-with-Em?gko=d33d3

Coopetition-based business models: The case of Amazon.com
http://www.sciencedirect.com/science/article/pii/S0019850113002150

The Effectiveness of Teamwork Training on Teamwork Behaviors and Team Performance: A Systematic Review and Meta-Analysis of Controlled Interventions, January 13, 2017
http://journals.plos.org/plosone/article?id=10.1371/journal.pone.0169604

Forbes SEP 21, 2017 @ 02:18 PM 7,458 The Little Black Book of Billionaire Secrets New Research: Diversity + Inclusion = Better Decision Making At Work
https://www.forbes.com/sites/eriklarson/2017/09/21/new-research-diversity-inclusion-better-decision-making-at-work/#5d1a0fa34cbf

Frenemies with Benefits
https://www.strategy-business.com/blog/Frenemies-with-Benefits?gko=358fc

HBR Does Diversity Actually Increase Creativity? Tomas Chamorro-Premuzic JUNE 28, 2017
https://hbr.org/2017/06/does-diversity-actually-increase-creativity

HBR: How Diversity Can Drive Innovation, Sylvia Ann Hewlett, Melinda Marshall, Laura Sherbin FROM THE DECEMBER 2013 ISSUE
https://hbr.org/2013/12/how-diversity-can-drive-innovation

How Does Diversity Spur Innovation? Research from Beyond Bias Summit Keynote Speaker Katherine W. Phillips reveals the connection
by Kristine Kilanski on Friday, March 24, 2017 - 3:22pm
http://gender.stanford.edu/news/2017/how-does-diversity-spur-innovation

How To Build a Coalition with the Coalition-Building Cycle
http://sourcesofinsight.com/coalition-building-cycle/

Inc. What Google's New Emotional Intelligence Study Says About Teamwork and Success Study backs up common experiences and provides insights into how to make teams work better.
https://www.inc.com/robin-camarote/google-study-reveals-emotional-intelligence-on-teams-determines-success.html

The Mix That Matters Innovation Through Diversity, APRIL 26, 2017
https://www.bcg.com/publications/2017/people-organization-leadership-talent-innovation-through-diversity-mix-that-matters.aspx

The New York Times. What Google Learned From Its Quest to Build the Perfect Team New research reveals surprising truths about why some work groups thrive and others falter. by Charles Duhigg, Feb. 25, 2016.
https://www.nytimes.com/2016/02/28/magazine/what-google-learned-from-its-quest-to-build-the-perfect-team.html

New Research Shows Why Focus On Teams, Not Just Leaders, Is Key To Business Performance
https://www.forbes.com/sites/joshbersin/2016/03/03/why-a-focus-on-teams-not-just-leaders-is-the-secret-to-business-performance/#7aa61aaa24d5

SHRM --Workplace Diversity and Inclusion Gets Innovative, Yesterday's workforce won't lead you into tomorrow by Novid Parsi, Jan 16, 2017
https://www.shrm.org/hr-today/news/hr-magazine/0217/pages/disrupting-diversity-in-the-workplace.aspx

Watkins, Michael (2003) 90 Days Critical Success Strategies for New Leaders at all Levels. Harvard Business Review Press, Boston.

> *The first most important, critical and strategic coalition in an individual's life is the coalition with one's own self.*
>
> — Sameh Elsayed

Chapter 8

Giving Back
How One Person Has the Potential to Build a Better World

Selected Quotes

" "

The only thing necessary for the triumph of evil is for good men to do nothing.

— Edmund Burke

Only a life lived for others is a life worthwhile.

— *Albert Einstein*

From what we get, we can make a living; what we give, however, makes a life.

— Arthur Ashe

To know even one life has breathed easier because you have lived. This is to have succeeded.

— Ralph Waldo Emerson

Life is a gift, and it offers us the privilege, opportunity, and responsibility to give something back by becoming more.

— Anthony Robbins

Give freely and become more wealthy; be stingy and lose everything.

— Proverbs 11:24-25

Give, and you will receive. Your gift will return to you in full—pressed down, shaken together to make room for more, running over, and poured into your lap. The amount you give will determine the amount you get back.

— Luke 6:38

Abstract

Giving back is engaging in activities that make a difference for others. The first action in giving back is to discover your sense of purpose, which provides a direction for all your important activities. Volunteerism is a very common form of giving back. Volunteerism provides many of the services for the needy in our community. Community advocacy is an advanced form of volunteerism that focuses on influencing policies, regulations, and elections in a democratic society. While giving back makes the community we live in a better place for generations to come, research studies also confirm numerous benefits for the person who gives back. Some of the benefits include: increased total health, longer life, increased happiness, and greater life fulfillment. Yes, giving back makes a real difference for others as well as for you.

Rate How Well You Give Back to Your Community

On a scale of 1 to 5, rate how well you give back by circling your choices
(1=Poor, 2=Below Average, 3=Average, 4=Good, 5=Excellent)

Your Level of Engagement	1= Poor 5= Excellent (Circle Your Choice)
1. You have discovered your sense of purpose.	1 2 3 4 5
2. Most of your career and personal activities support your sense of purpose.	1 2 3 4 5
3. You volunteer in at least one cause that benefits others.	1 2 3 4 5
4. Your volunteer activities are balanced with the rest of your life.	1 2 3 4 5
5. You are actively engaged in community advocacy.	1 2 3 4 5
6. Your community advocacy activities are balanced with the rest of your life.	1 2 3 4 5
7. You engage in conversations about matters you have some control over.	1 2 3 4 5
8. You engage in conversations where you are either learning from others or sharing insights.	1 2 3 4 5
9. You properly manage a balance between your community and you personal commitments.	1 2 3 4 5
10. You have direct experience with the benefits of giving back to the community.	1 2 3 4 5

Your total score is _____

Assess your score:

40 +	Outstanding
30 +	Very Good
25 +	Good
Below 25	Needs Improvement

Giving Back Success Story

Note: The purpose of this story is to illustrate the application of principles and skills covered in this chapter. The story is based on character elements of real people I know personally, but the details and events are my creative work designed for illustrative purposes.

Tebabu is an exemplary community advocate. His community advocacy is based on the greater good for many and diverse groups of people. He has been working on a benefit corporation growth model that benefits people of two continents (the USA and the continent of Africa). Tebabu and his wife Sara own Blessed Coffee Corporation, which is based on the benefit corporation model. This allows Tebabu to practice what he preaches.

The benefit corporate growth model allows job creators of the USA and the continent of Africa to do business with one another for mutually beneficial outcomes. Tebebu works both aisles of the US Congress to obtain congressional support. His volunteers are very dedicated to the mission and represent diverse and eclectic backgrounds. Tebabu gives a talk to community groups on the subject of community advocacy and giving back to the community.

When you speak with Tebabu, here are his recurring messages:

"While I understand the work I do is important and it is going to make a difference, I am not doing this alone. My entire family is totally behind this effort. I am also blessed with all the dedicated volunteers who make our efforts a reality."

"We are enjoying the journey of this initiative. In transformation work, the process is as important as the desired outcome."

"If you want to see the world around you look and act a certain way, you must work to create it."

"The new business model is doing good for the common good and doing well for yourself."

"If your cause is worthy, focus by putting both your hands on it when you work on your cause and talk to people about it, talk and act like you are winning."

Tebabu is so excited about his cause of creating the benefit corporation that benefits America and Africa, when he talks about it, his joy is contagious. If you know Tebabu, you will be certain to hear about the benefit corporation and you will soon be his fan and become an expert on the subject.

Success Story Discussion Questions

Do you think Tebabu is a successful person? Why?

What is one thing about Tebabu that you like the most?

What is your prediction of Tebabu's efforts in 5- 7 years ?

Giving Back- Introduction

Giving back to your community is the decision and practice of making the world a better place for others. Giving back may begin with:

- One random act of kindness

- One person who needs your help

- A community that benefits from your action

We are all created to be equal but different. This means, each of us have different talents, interests, and different levels of commitment. Thus, giving back will be different for different people.

Giving back to your community takes three general forms: discovering your sense of purpose, engaging in volunteerism, and community advocacy.

The Three Axis of Giving Back to Your Community

A Sense of Purpose

A desire to achieve something that is important to you, as well as a desire to make a difference in the world. Making a difference to the world begins with something as simple as making a difference to someone in your family as well as doing something that affects the lives of lots of other people. The point is that purpose is about more than just ourselves - it's also about having a positive impact on the lives of others in some way.

Volunteerism

The practice of volunteering one's time or talents for charitable, educational, or other worthwhile activities, especially in one's community.

Community Advocacy

Community advocacy is an activity by an individual or group which aims to influence decisions within political, economic, and social systems and institutions.

Discovering Your Sense of Purpose

A sense of purpose means having something in your life that is so meaningful to you that you don't want to give it up. It's something that without you might not be achieved or accomplished. A sense of purpose is something that will inspire you to a greater level of achievement.

We may have one strong purpose in life, like to be a great teacher or to work for the welfare of animals or to bring up children successfully. This one strong purpose may steer the course of our life.

We may have several different purposes at the same time, such as being a good parent, loving others, being helpful by the work that we do, and giving, in some way, to our local community. Or we may have different purposes at different times in our lives depending on our age and family circumstances.

Examples of Statements of Sense of Purpose

Here is a list of examples of statements of sense of purpose. Your sense of purpose may align with one of these examples. Better yet, you may use these examples as a guide to develop your own statement of sense of purpose.

My sense of purpose is:

- To restore old cars and find original parts for those who love to do the same. I will hunt down, collect, organize and stock hard to find parts and resell them -- as well as offer expert advice on auto restoration and valuations.

- To help online business owners be fully booked by using my web design and SEO skills to make sure customers and clients can find them online.

- To capture the special events of weddings, anniversaries, and graduations and turn them into memories with photographs and videos that highlight those special moments and behind the scenes which make each event unique.

- To help develop and test formulas to reduce acne and the effects of sun damage on young and aging skin.

- To write and produce songs that speak to the human connection across cultures; thereby, creating appreciation and closeness among all people.

- To make people feel beautiful by cutting and styling their hair in a way that expresses who they are and where they are going in life. Drawing on years of experience, I will work on creating innovative cuts that show off the best features of my clients.

- To create strong female anime characters and storylines that empower women to become great and not fear their own power to change lives. I will use my creativity, graphic design, and animating skills to develop sketches and storyboards for film, comic books, and online videos.

- To be a spokesman for wildlife issues and help people connect their daily actions to saving the wildlife on this planet.

- To teach underprivileged children the keys to success and how to become young and successful entrepreneurs by igniting their ambition to change their lives.

- To learn how to use humor and kindness to help people adjust to the inevitable changes that come with aging and ill health.

- To help people find the love of their lives, that one person in the Universe who gets them. I love to bring people together, read chemistry, and make love come alive.

- To grow nutritious, organic food that helps people grow and thrive and have vibrant health. I want to use my skills as a grower to build a sustainable farm that educates as well as feeds people, and builds a community of like-minded organic growers and consumers.

- To create an online voice for autism to educate parents, teachers, and patients about the latest developments and coping strategies. I want to use my skills of planning, researching, and heralding to help direct funding to the most promising research and share those developments with those who need to know.

- To raise awareness about the effects of smoking and drop the rate of new smokers by 50% in the next 5 years. Using my talent for creating ad copy, humorous viral campaigns, and mob flashes – I want to get the word out that smoking is not cool. And I want to work with tobacco companies to introduce non addictive smoking alternatives (herbal cigarettes, etc.) so those that do smoke will have a healthier alternative like they use on Mad Men.

- To build awesome custom bikes that win mountain bike and speed competitions. I will use my talent for design, prototyping, and customizing to dream up, develop, test, refine, build, and sell world class cycling equipment.

- To help distressed homeowners refinance their mortgages and become better financial consumers by understanding the real details behind home buying, credit ratings and approvals, and secured debt. I want to use my analysis and coaching skills to help people stay in their homes and keep their dream of owning their own home alive.

- To work to reduce teen suicides caused by bullying and a lack of self-worth. I want to help teenagers discover that being different is OK and create hope when they feel their life is crashing down around them and nobody will understand what they are going through.

- To change the way we interact online and bring civility to the Internet through workshops, articles, and being a spokesperson for civility on the Internet. I want to consult with major companies and colleges to increase awareness of what is bad behavior and the effects it can have on ruining lives.

- To create plays and stories that help illuminate ancient wisdom and bring to light some of the great, universal themes covered by Shakespeare, Milton, and the Greek playwrights – but updated for modern audiences.

- To design and build beautiful wood desks, elegant computer cabinets, and amazing dining tables. I will use my eye for detail, my intuitive sense of old world styling and craftsmanship to make custom furniture that evokes traditional styles with modern functionality.

Written Activity

What are 3-5 statements that you may relate to or may benefit from their accomplishments.

Write your own statement of purpose and discuss with others.

Benefits of Discovering a Sense of Purpose

Research has shown that having a sense of moral purpose is really important for our happiness and emotional wellbeing. Our purpose keeps us motivated, gives us energy, and helps us cope with any problems or difficult circumstances that come up. Purpose is also about recognizing and fulfilling our highest potential, allowing us to be our best and give our best to others.

Victor Frankl initiated research into purpose and meaning, with his book, *Man's Search for Meaning.*

Frankl was a Jewish psychiatrist who experienced and survived life as a prisoner in the Nazi concentration camps during World War II. In his book he describes his experience and his observations of how life could be endured, even in these worst possible circumstances. He explained that this can be done by having a strong desire to find a meaning or purpose. Some prisoners were committed to the purpose of surviving for someone they loved who they believed was still alive.

Frankl, like others, was committed to the purpose of providing care and support to those even worse off than himself in the camp.

Frankl also had an even greater purpose – he believed his experience could help people suffering from anxiety and stress, by helping them to find their purpose in life. He suggested that to be truly happy, we need a sense of purpose or meaning that is outside of ourselves. And that when we lose sight of our purpose or worth to others, we become anxious and stressed. After his time in the camp, he went on to help people in his therapeutic practice to discover what they valued most and reach their true potential.

Living and acting with others' interests at heart without obvious benefit to ourselves has been shown to be good for our health and wellbeing. Research shows that helping others can boost our confidence and our immune system.

Having a strong moral purpose has been found to give meaning to life in the here and now as well as the future. It can also promote mental well being, achievement, and prosocial behavior (behavior that shows concern for the welfare of others).

Not having a sense of purpose can leave us without a sense of direction or with a sense of confusion about our lives and therefore a lack of fulfilment. If we let ourselves be led along in the flow of life around us, we may not end up where we want to be. Having a strong sense of purpose helps us direct and take control of our own lives and our own destinies.

Having A Sense Of Purpose Can Reduce Anxiety

Having a sense of purpose can combat daily stress and anxiety, according to research done by Anthony Burrow, Assistant Professor of Human Development in the College of Human Ecology at Cornell. Surveying passengers on Chicago trains, Burrows held two studies where participants reported their mood as they traveled. In one study, commuters assessed their life purpose through a short questionnaire before they boarded the train.

The second study had half of the participants partake in a questionnaire about movies, while the other half completed a writing exercise about life purpose. Negative moods were reported more frequently when train cars grew increasingly crowded and diverse. Heightened feelings of anxiety and stress were not experienced, however, for those who reported a sense of life purpose. These results were found in both studies.

"There is evidence that focusing on personally meaningful and valued goals can buffer the negative effects of stress by allowing individuals to reinforce a sense of who they are," Burrows shared with the public. Findings from the Americans' Changing Lives Studies (ACL), an ongoing project that has been observing the lives of American adults since 1986, agree. Researchers of this long-term study found that in two groups separated by those who volunteer and those who do not, the group that gave back had higher levels of self-esteem and overall life satisfaction.

Giving to a larger purpose to attain a happier life makes sense for the average person, but what about those who combat an anxiety disorder or suffer from another mental illness? Mark Musick and John Wilson of the University of Texas asked the same questions when conducting research that built on the ACL study. They found that volunteering also lowered depression, adding to a phenomenon that has been dubbed 'the activism cure.' "Volunteer work improves access to social and psychological resources, which are known to counter negative moods," Musick reported.

How to develop a sense of purpose

In affirming your purpose in life, you answer the following questions:

1) Where are you going with your life?

2) What kind of person do you want to be?

3) What can you contribute to others?

These are questions about your purpose in life. They are sometimes difficult questions, depending on where we are in our lives. But evidence suggests strongly that having answers to these questions will help us flourish.

Yes! You are a Model Volunteer

As a Volunteer, You are Already at the Top. Here is How you Stay up There

Selected Quotes

Service to others is the rent you pay for your room here on Earth.

— Muhammad Ali

Volunteers do not necessarily have the time; they just have the heart.

— Elizabeth Andrew

If our hopes of building a better and safer world are to become more than wishful thinking, we will need the engagement of volunteers more than ever.

— Kofi Annan

What is the essence of life? To serve others and to do good.

— Aristotle

We have to do what we can to help wherever and whenever it is possible for us to help.

— Jackie Chan

We make a living by what we get, but we make a life by what we give.

— Winston Churchill

Yes! You are a Model Volunteer

As a volunteer, you are already at the top. Here is how you stay up there. This list also include actions that an organization must take to remain the best destination for volunteers.

1. *Are you making a difference?* Regularly ask yourself: Is this volunteer opportunity aligned with my life purpose? Am I making a difference?

What the organization must ask and do: Is this volunteer engaged for the right reasons? Regularly conduct volunteer onboarding.

2. *Are you working on the right priority items?* Constantly prioritize your volunteer activities. Remember, you must be the driver of your life boat.

What the organization must ask and do: Is the organization constantly communicating its priorities? Be supportive when the priorities of the volunteer change.

3. *Are you excited about the mission of the organization?* Only volunteer when your heart is in the mission of the organization you are supporting. If you do not believe in the mission, leave the organization immediately. Do not attempt to change the mission of the organization. The organization serves a good societal purpose.

What the organization must ask and do: Do you monitor volunteer experiences? Always communicate organizational mission.

4. *Are you transparent?* Communicate always. You must communicate when your priorities change, your status changes, and you encounter challenges and successes.

What the organization must ask and do: Does the organization demonstrate transparency? Incentivize open communication by appreciating authentic communication.

5. *Are you injecting positive energy?* Maintain positive energy with others. Other volunteers need positive energy to be successful. Stay far away from gossip and hearsay. These breed toxic energy. Choose to be a source of positive energy.

What the organization must ask and do: Is the organization a place where volunteers feel emotionally safe? Foster a culture of assuming good intent.

6. *Are you helpful?* Offer help to other volunteers. Seek help when you need it. Most of the help sought is psychological and emotional in nature and does not cost you anything.

What the organization must ask and do: Are people celebrated or tolerated? Foster a trusting environment.

7. *Do you freely say "No" without excuses?* Politely decline when you are unable to make a commitment. Refrain from volunteering others to fulfil an assignment you are not able to perform.

What the organization must ask and do: Do "Yes" and "No" responses get equal treatment? Accept "No" responses as good gifts.

8. *Are you proactive?* Be proactive in providing the status of your assignments. Do not wait until you are constantly reminded. Remember, your colleagues are counting on you to do your part.

What the organization must ask and do: Are status meetings regularly scheduled? Status meetings are opportunities to find out where volunteers are and what help they may need.

9. *Do you get things done?* Complete your assignment end to end. Every assignment has three phases: preparation phase, execution phase, and follow up phase. Be present to complete the assignment from preparation to follow up.

What the organization must ask and do: Are volunteers empowered? Set volunteers up as process owners.

10. *Do you improve your game?* Seek feedback on your role and assignments from time to time. Seeking and incorporating feedback improves the quality of your services and the organization as a whole.

What the organization must ask and do: Are mistakes and errors welcomed? Foster a culture of excellence over perfection.

11. *Do you move on when it is time?* While volunteering in general is a necessary life practice, volunteering in one organization cannot be a lifelong commitment. Change is a life blood of organizational vitality. Thus, you must plan your exit strategy and timing. Communicate in advance of your exit so that your successor can be assigned.

What the organization must ask and do: Do we want to be dynamic or stagnant? Schedule regular send off parties and celebrations.

Introduction

The prime purpose of "Yes! You are a model volunteer" is to help volunteers realize how special they are as volunteers and how they can remain special. This section presents guidelines that help volunteers stay at the top of their game.

The secondary purpose of "Yes! You are a model volunteer" is to help organizations who host volunteers to create and foster the right organizational climate to remain a good home for volunteers.

The purpose of volunteering is to make a positive difference in the lives of people and in society. Volunteers must be very deliberate in choosing the right volunteer opportunity to ensure they are at the right place at the right time. Organizations must also attract and retain volunteers who are likely to advance their mission.

General Volunteer Opportunities

Here are examples of available volunteer opportunities. One of these volunteer opportunities may suit your interest. The list may also inspire you to have a volunteer venture of your own. Check the items that interest you based on your life purpose:

_____ 1. Donating your expertise and doing a few hours of community service for free.

_____ 2. Tutoring students for free.

_____ 3. Teaching others what you know at a library or community organization, or working pro bono.

_____ 4. Most homeless shelters welcome volunteers and have a variety of programs through which you can get involved. You might help prepare or distribute meals, work behind the scenes in the business office, help organize a food drive to stock the pantry, etc.

_____ 5. Special Olympics is an international program of year-round sports training and athletic competition for children and adults with mental retardation. Volunteer activities include: sports training, fundraising, administrative help, competition planning and staffing, etc.

_____ 6. Habitat for Humanities builds and gives houses to poor people in local communities. Volunteers not only help others but can learn a great deal about building houses by getting involved.

_____7. Many state parks have volunteer programs, and in these programs you can try anything from educational programs to trail construction and maintenance.

_____8. Reading is one of the most important skills an adult can have; however, many adults have never learned to read. Literacy volunteers act as tutors who help illiterate children and adults learn this important skill.

_____9. Many hospitals have volunteer programs to help patients both inside and outside the hospital. The volunteers programs allow participants to explore medical careers and gain work experience.

_____10. Many senior citizen centers offer volunteer programs to provide friendship and community activities to senior citizens. If you would like working with senior citizens, call a senior citizen center in your neighborhood and see what kinds of volunteer programs are available.

_____10. Many animal shelters are nonprofit or government organizations, and therefore they welcome volunteers to help take care of animals, keep facilities clean, and work with the public. Call a local animal shelter for more information.

_____11. The United Way is a nationwide umbrella organization for thousands of charitable organizations. The United Way raises billions of dollars and distributes it to these charities. There are local United Way affiliates across the country and they need volunteers. Contact your local affiliate for more information.

_____12. The American Red Cross helps people in emergencies – ranging from half a million disaster victims to one sick child who needs blood. Volunteer opportunities exist across the country. Contact your local Red Cross for more information.

_____13. The Salvation Army provides social services, rehabilitation centers, disaster services, worship opportunities, and character building groups and activities for all ages. Volunteer opportunities exist across the country.

_____14. The Sierra Club (and numerous other environmental groups) encourages volunteer support to help with environmental activities. You can help in many ways: by lobbying on conservation issues, by leading hikes and other activities, or by lending a hand at the chapter office.

_____15. In an election year, there are thousands of opportunities to volunteer in political campaigns around the country. You can learn more than you imagine by getting involved in politics. Pick a candidate whose ideas you believe in (either on the local, state, or national level) and volunteer to be a part of his or her campaign.

Written Activity

What are the top 3-5 volunteer opportunities from the list, where you want to make a difference in your lifetime?

Write your dream volunteer activity and explain why it appeals to you.

Benefits of Volunteering

Volunteering comes with benefits for all involved.

According to the Corporation for National Community Services, the biggest benefit people get from volunteering is the satisfaction of incorporating service into their lives and making a difference in their community and country.

The intangible benefits of pride, satisfaction, and accomplishment are worthwhile reasons to serve. In addition, when we share our time and talents we solve problems, strengthen communities, improve lives, connect to others, and transform our own lives.

There is a growing body of research which indicates volunteering provides individual health benefits. A report titled: *The Health Benefits of Volunteering: A Review of Recent Research*, presented by the Corporation for National Community Service, established a strong relationship between volunteering and health – those who volunteer have lower mortality rates, greater functional ability, and lower rates of depression later in life than those who do not volunteer.

Comparisons of the health benefits of volunteering for different age groups have also shown that older volunteers are the most likely to receive greater benefits from volunteering, whether because they are more likely to face higher incidence of illness or because volunteering provides them with physical and social activity and a sense of purpose at a time when their social roles are changing.

Some of these findings also indicate that volunteers who devote a "considerable" amount of time to volunteer activities (about 100 hours per year) are most likely to exhibit positive health outcomes.

Volunteering and the happiness effect

Helping others kindles happiness, as many studies have demonstrated. When researchers at the London School of Economics examined the relationship between volunteering and measures of happiness in a large group of American adults, they found that the more people volunteered, the happier they were, according to a study in *Social Science and Medicine*.

Compared with people who never volunteered, the odds of being "very happy" rose 7% among those who volunteer monthly and 12% for people who volunteer every two to four weeks. Among weekly volunteers, 16% felt very happy – a hike in happiness comparable to having an income of $75,000-$100,000 versus $20,000, say the researchers.

Volunteering can advance your career

According to Help Guide, a trusted guide to mental, emotional, and social health, volunteering can help you get experience in your area of interest and meet people in the field.

Even if you're not planning on changing careers, volunteering gives you the opportunity to practice important skills used in the workplace, such as teamwork, communication, problem solving, project planning, task management, and organization. You might feel more comfortable stretching your wings at work once you've honed these skills in a volunteer position first.

Primary Considerations for choosing the right volunteer opportunity

Choosing the right volunteer opportunity starts with acknowledgement of your life purpose.

Your name (Jeremy):
1. What is one word that best describes you? (Jeremy's example:improver)

2. What is your claim to fame or what are you known for? (Jeremy's example: if it ain't broke, you are not trying hard enough)

3. What is your life purpose (Jeremy's example: Service above self)

Secondary Considerations for Choosing the right volunteer opportunity

1. Would you like to work with adults, children, or animals?

2. Do you prefer to work alone or as part of a team? Would you prefer remotely from home?

3. Are you better behind the scenes or do you prefer to take a more visible role?

4. How much time (per day or week or month or year) are you willing to commit?

5. What skills can you bring to a volunteer job?

6. What causes are important to you?

Based on your responses to primary and secondary considerations, write down your volunteer plan. In other words, write down the volunteer opportunity of your choice including role and level of commitment.

Are you ready to volunteer?

Which of the following reasons listed below cause you to sign up as a volunteer? (check all that apply)

_____You attend an event and you really like the people behind the event. You want to be on that team.

_____Organizers of an event you attend make a persuasive pitch and sound desperate for volunteers

_____The mission of an organization is consistent with your career or life goals and you want to volunteer.

_____Other reasons, if any?

Do you have the bandwidth (attention) to volunteer?

What is your disposable time to volunteer?

What are your current volunteer commitments/engagements?

How well are you performing on your current volunteer commitments/engagements?

How many other volunteer commitments do you have?

Do your family commitments allow you time to volunteer?

Does your work schedule allow you to volunteer?

Are you emotionally ready to volunteer?

Are you physically ready to volunteer?

What are the requirements of the volunteer opportunity/organization?

What are the time requirements?

What are the skill requirements?

What are the temperament requirements?

What is the organization culture?

Do you know the time requirements of a volunteer opportunity? Do you know the skills requirements of a volunteer opportunity? Do you know the temperament requirement of a volunteer opportunity? Do you know the organizational culture of the volunteer seeking organization?

Written Activity

Suppose Go Pro21 Community seeks your volunteer engagement:

(1) What are your reasons to volunteer?

(2) What is your time availability?

(3) Explain the requirements of volunteering?

(4) What are your terms and conditions for volunteering?

Restating your Case to Volunteer?

How does volunteering benefit you? (Examples: the fulfillment of giving back, building a good reputation, getting good career referral, acquiring skills and knowledge. etc)

How does volunteering benefit the organization? (Examples: accomplishing mission, saving money, etc)

How does volunteering benefit the community? (Examples: economic development, job creation, safe neighborhoods, child safety, etc.)

Rate Your Current Success as Volunteer

On a scale of 1 to 5, rate how well you serve as a volunteer by circling your choices (1=Poor, 2=Below Average, 3=Average, 4=Good, 5=Excellent)

Your Level of Success as a Volunteer	1= Poor 5= Excellent (Circle Your Choice)
1. Your reason for volunteering with this organization is clear to you and to the target organization.	1 2 3 4 5
2. You have adequate time to dedicate to this organization.	1 2 3 4 5
3. You constantly prioritize your role and assignments.	1 2 3 4 5
4. You and the target organization have mutually agreed on your role and assignments.	1 2 3 4 5
5. When necessary, you seek clarification about your role and assignments.	1 2 3 4 5
6. When necessary, you seek to renegotiate your role and assignments.	1 2 3 4 5
7. When necessary, you seek clarification of what is expected of you.	1 2 3 4 5
8. After completion of assignments, you seek and obtain feedback about your performance.	1 2 3 4 5
9. You are generally satisfied with your volunteer engagement.	1 2 3 4 5
10. As a result of your volunteer role and assignments, you feel like you are making a positive difference in the lives of people and contributing to society.	1 2 3 4 5

Your total score is _____

Assess your score:

40 +	Outstanding
30 +	Very Good
25 +	Good
Below 25	Needs Improvement

Concluding Remarks

Yes! You are indeed a Model Volunteer. As a volunteer, you are already at the top. You stay up there by affirmatively answering these questions:

As a Volunteer	As an Organization
• Are you making a difference? Regularly ask yourself: Is this volunteer opportunity aligned with your life purpose?	• Is this volunteer engaged for the right reasons?
• Are you working on the right priority items?	• Is the organization constantly communicating its priorities?
• Are you excited about the mission of the organization?	• Do you monitor volunteer experiences?
• Are you transparent?	• Does the organization demonstrate transparency?
• Are you injecting positive energy?	• Is the organization a place where volunteers feel emotionally safe?
• Are you helpful?	• Are people celebrated or tolerated?
• Do you freely say "No" without excuses.	• Do "Yes" and "No" get equal treatment?
• Are you proactive?	• Are status meetings regularly scheduled?
• Do you get things done?	• Are volunteers empowered?
• Do you improve your game?	• Are mistakes and errors welcomed?
• Do you move on when it is time?	• Do we want to be dynamic or stagnant?

Advocacy Groups

Advocacy is speaking, acting, and/or writing with minimal conflict of interest on behalf of the sincerely perceived interests of a disadvantaged person or group to promote, protect and defend their welfare and justice by: being on their side and no-one else's; being primarily concerned with their fundamental needs; remaining loyal and accountable to them in a way which is emphatic and vigorous and which is, or is likely to be, costly to the advocate or advocacy group.

Examples of Advocacy Groups

The Southern Poverty Law Center is a non-profit advocacy organization that focuses on civil rights. Founded in 1971 by Morris Dees and Joseph Levin Jr., the Southern Poverty Law Center ("SPLC") began as a law firm working on behalf of people who were victims of hate crimes. The group gained a reputation in its victories against white supremacy groups, such as the Ku Klux Klan. Over the years, as the advocacy organization expanded, it became involved in other civil rights cases, including those concerned with gender-based discrimination, mistreatment of immigrants, and segregation. The SPLC has worked closely with other organizations, including the Anti-Defamation League, in its civil rights journey.

Unite Oregon (formerly known as Center for Intercultural Organizing in Portland, OR) is led by people of color, immigrants and refugees, rural communities, and people experiencing poverty, and works across Oregon to build a unified intercultural movement for justice. Unite Oregon represents the merger of two strong organizations – Center for Intercultural Organizing (CIO) and Oregon Action (OA) – who together have decades of experience organizing immigrants, refugees, people of color, and low-income Oregonians to address racial and economic disparities and improve quality of life in the state of Oregon.

CASA de Maryland is a Latino and immigration advocacy-and-assistance organization based in Maryland. CASA is dedicated to creating a more just society by building power and improving the quality of life in low-income immigrant communities. Stated vision of CASA is a future with diverse and thriving communities living free from discrimination and fear, working together with mutual respect to achieve full human rights for all.

Tea Party Patriots is a conservative American political organization that promotes fiscally responsible activism as part of the Tea Party movement. Its mission is "to attract, educate, organize, and mobilize our fellow citizens to secure public policy consistent with our three core values of Fiscal Responsibility, Constitutionally Limited Government and Free Markets." The group is a strong opponent of "excess" government spending and debt. The organization was founded by Jenny Beth Martin, Mark Meckler, and Amy Kremer in March 2009. Tea Party Patriots is most notable for organizing citizen opposition at the health care town hall meetings of 2009, as well as various other anti-government run health care protests.

EMILY's List is an American political action committee (PAC) that aims to help elect pro-choice Democratic female candidates to office. It was founded by Ellen Malcolm in 1985. The group's name is an acronym for "Early Money Is Like Yeast".   The saying is a reference to a convention of political fundraising that receiving lots of donations early in a race is helpful in attracting subsequent donors. Emily's List bundles contributions to the campaigns of pro-choice Democratic women running in targeted races.

The Club for Growth is a conservative organization active in the United States, with an agenda focused on cutting taxes and other economic issues. The Club has two political arms: an affiliated traditional political action committee, called the Club for Growth PAC, and Club for Growth Action, an independent-expenditure only committee or Super-PAC. The Club for Growth's policy goals include cutting income tax rates, repealing the estate tax, supporting limited government and a balanced budget amendment, entitlement reform, free trade, tort reform, school choice, and deregulation. The Club for Growth PAC endorses and raises money for candidates who meet its standards for fiscal conservatism.

Benefits of Advocacy

Benefits of Engaging in Grassroots Advocacy

- You can effectively influence policy and potentially shape the direction of an issue of your interest.

- You have the opportunity to educate and engage your community members with information that directly impacts their interests.

- You have the opportunity to innovate and make a positive impact on the direction of your community.

- You have the opportunity to facilitate social or regulatory changes that will benefit your community.

- You have the prospect of increasing awareness regarding community related issues and problems.

- You have the guarantee that your voice and opinions will be heard by policy makers.

- You have the chance to make a real difference in the lives of your community members.

- All members can contact their legislators directly without filters or watering down their own personal message and thoughts.

Best Practices in Advocacy

Start Regular, Personal Communications.

You should contact policy makers every month or two, by email or telephone.

Write letters-to-the-editor about issues.

Members of Congress always read the letters in their hometown newspapers. Editors like letters that respond to something that appeared recently in the paper. Keep your letter concise, approximately 150 words. Most newspapers prefer email submissions. Include your full name, address, phone number, and email.

Attend town hall meetings.

Attend town hall meetings that your members of Congress hold and ask questions about the issues you are advocating. You may also make an appointment to meet with your member of Congress in the local office. Don't forget the state and county fairs that politicians frequent on weekends and during the August Congressional recess. Tell about the potential impact locally of proposed legislation (positive or negative), or tell about the ways that funding shortfalls have hurt the local service deliverers.

Invite your members of Congress to visit your organization.
If one accepts, you can show off your work, but also ask some direct questions about what they are doing in Congress that supports your work.

Build relationships with Congressional staff

Congressional staff work in the state or local offices (District Offices). They represent the member of Congress at local meetings and events, and serve as caseworkers to help constituents with federal programs and benefits. Invite them to regular meetings and events on your calendar, and let them know how you can help them serve the community. Then when the Senator or Representative needs to know how legislation might affect constituents, local staff will know who to turn to for input.

Share information and ideas with others in your community

Partner with others who care about your issues, perhaps starting or contributing to a listserv on issues.

Checklist of Giving Back Activities

____ Do I believe in the people I serve and show it with expressed love, kind words, and respect?

____ Do I really know and understand my target audience in terms of their strengths and their challenges?

____ Do I prioritize and focus my energy and attention on targeted causes I believe in with a realization that my energy and attention are only useful when concentrated?

____ Do I realize God loves a cheerful giver, thus, smile and ensure the heart behind the Giving is totally in support of the act.

____ Do I understand Adam Grant's principles of givers and takers, where the cardinal rule is "Givers are Winners?"

____ Do I value people who "show me how to fish" more than the people "who give me fish for one meal?

____ Do I practice readily saying "Yes, Gladly" or "No, Thanks" to requests of all kinds I receive with 20% "Yes" and 80% "No"

_____ Do I rotate the causes I support and lead every other year with an understanding that there are other people who can potentially do this better than I do?

_____ Do I identify the sector of the larger audience to seek support and to serve with an understanding of realistically being able to reach only 4 - 7% of the total targeted audience?

_____ Do I know when it is time to join and support others versus starting my own cause with an understanding that fantastic followers are amazing leaders?

Closing Remarks

Giving back is engaging in activities that make a difference for others. The first action in giving back is to discover your sense of purpose, which provides a direction for all your important activities. Volunteerism is a very common form of giving back. Volunteerism provides many of the services for the needy in our community. Community advocacy is an advanced form of volunteerism that focuses on influencing policies, regulations, and elections in a democratic society. While giving back makes the community we live in a better place for generations to come, research studies also confirm numerous benefits for the person who gives back. Some of the benefits includes: increased total health, longer life, increased happiness, and greater life fulfillment. Yes, giving back makes a real difference for others as well as for you.

End of Chapter Activity

1. *What is a statement of your purpose in life?*

2. *What are your major volunteer accomplishments?*

3. *What are your potential future volunteer activity goals?*

4. *What advocacy groups do you wish to support or launch?*

References

http://www.manifestyourpotential.com/self_discovery/5_discover_life_purpose/statement_examples_of_life_purpose.htm

http://www.handsonscotland.co.uk/flourishing_and_wellbeing_in_children_and_young_people/sense_of_purpose/sense_of_purpose.html

https://www.anxiety.org/how-having-a-sense-of-purpose-can-reduce-anxiety

http://www.bygpub.com/books/tg2rw/volunteer.htm

https://www.nationalservice.gov/serve-your-community/benefits-volunteering
https://www.nationalservice.gov/pdf/07_0506_hbr.pdf

http://www.health.harvard.edu/special-health-reports/simple-changes-big-rewards-a-practical-easy-guide-for-healthy-happy-living

http://www.helpguide.org/articles/work-career/volunteering-and-its-surprising-benefits.htm

http://articles.salsalabs.com/advocacy-definition/

http://qla.org.au/~qlaorg/PDFforms/Advocacy%20Info.pdf

It's enough to indulge and to be selfish but true happiness is really when you start giving back.

— Adrian Grenier

Chapter 9

Excellence Over Perfection
How Perfection is the Enemy of Good

Selected Quotes

" "

If you wait for perfect conditions, you will not get anything done.

— Ecclesiastes 11: 4

We are what we repeatedly do. Excellence, then, is not an act, but a habit.

— Aristotle

Excellence is openness to being wrong. Perfection is having to be right.

— Greenspon

I am careful not to confuse excellence with perfection. Excellence, I can reach for. Perfect is God's business.

— Michael J. Fox

Perfectionism is self-abuse of the highest order.

— Ann Wilson Shaef

Excellence is encouraging. Perfectionism is criticizing.

— Greenspon

When perfectionism is driving us, shame is always riding shotgun and fear is the back seat driver.

— Brene Brown

Perfectionism leads to procrastination which leads to paralysis...and the cycle continues.

— unknown

Abstract

"Perfection is the enemy of good" seems counterintuitive but refers to the fact that often people freeze when trying to accomplish important tasks due to not having perfect circumstances. Ecclesiastes 11: 4 instructs, "If you wait for perfect conditions, you will not get anything done." Based on extensive research findings, this chapter advocates that you may benefit from the pursuit of excellence rather than the pursuit of perfection.

Perfection is expecting oneself or others to produce a desired outcome during the first attempt; while excellence is iteratively working toward producing a valuable outcome. Some terms that are associated with the concept of perfection are: stressful, to impress, inflexible, intolerant, doubt, judgmental, and control. Some words that are associated with excellence are: useful, improve, iterate, flexible, confidence, and dynamic. Perfectionist behaviors have been the subject of extensive research. Some of the consequences of perfectionist behavior include: performance anxiety, burn-out, depression, eating disorders, and even suicide.

Perfectionism is a combination of exceedingly high standards and a preoccupation with extreme self-critical evaluation. Perfectionism has multidimensional traits including perfectionistic strivings and perfectionistic concerns. Perfectionistic strivings include positive emotional experiences, active coping strategies and greater performance. Perfectionistic concerns are associated with an array of maladaptive outcomes. These include almost the converse of perfectionistic strivings such as greater appraisals, anxiety, and avoidant coping.

Perfectionistic Concerns vs. Perfectionistic Strivings

Perfectionism/Perfectionistic Concerns	Perfectionistic Striving/Healthy Striving
<ul><li>standards are beyond reach and reason</li><li>Never satisfied by anything less than perfection</li><li>depressed when faced with failure or disappointment</li><li>Preoccupied with fears of failure and disapproval</li><li>Seeing mistakes as unworthiness</li><li>Becoming overly defensive when criticized</li></ul>	<ul><li>standards are high but within reach</li><li>Enjoy process and outcome</li><li>Bounce back quickly from failure or disappointment</li><li>normal anxiety and fear of failure within bounds</li><li>See mistakes as opportunities for growth and learning</li><li>Reacting positively to helpful criticism</li></ul>

Coping strategies to turn from perfectionist behavior to the pursuit of excellence include:

- Increase your awareness of the self-critical nature of your all or nothing thoughts, and how they extend to other people in your life.

- Be realistic about what you can do. By setting more realistic goals, you will gradually realize that "imperfect" results do not lead to the punitive consequences you expect and fear.

- Set strict time limits on each of your projects. When the time is up, move on to another activity.

- Learn how to deal with criticism. Perfectionists often view criticism as a personal attack, which leads them to respond defensively.

While perfectionism is likely to jeopardize the wellbeing of individual contributors, teams, and organizations, the pursuit of excellence is likely to benefit all involved.

Rate Your Current Level of Excellence Over Perfection
(1=Poor, 2=Below Average, 3=Average, 4=Good, 5=Excellent)

Excellence Over Perfection Actions	1= Poor 5= Excellent (Circle Your Choice)
1. You set standards that are high but within reach.	1 2 3 4 5
2. You enjoy process as well as outcome.	1 2 3 4 5
3. You bounce back quickly from failure or disappointment.	1 2 3 4 5
4. You keep normal anxiety or fear of failure within bounds.	1 2 3 4 5
5. You see mistakes as opportunities for growth and learning.	1 2 3 4 5
6. You create joyful moments in your work.	1 2 3 4 5
7. You celebrate small achievements.	1 2 3 4 5
8. You give credit to those who help you along the way.	1 2 3 4 5
9. You weigh all inputs with an open mind.	1 2 3 4 5
10. You welcome making early stage mistakes.	1 2 3 4 5

Your total score is _____

Assess your score:

40 +	Outstanding
30 +	Very Good
25 +	Good
Below 25	Needs Improvement

Excellence Over Perfection Success Story

Note: The purpose of this story is to illustrate the application of principles and skills covered in this chapter. The story is based on character elements of real people I know personally, but the details and events are my creative work designed for illustrative purposes.

Jonathan is president of Wild Horizons, a boutique coaching practice. He possesses diverse skills such as instructional design, project management, technical writing, training delivery, coaching, graphics design, and leadership development. Jonathan gets a lot done in a very short period of time with great precision, excellence, and with minimal stress.

Here are Jonathan's secrets:

- He takes on multiple client assignments.

- He starts all his assignments at the same time.

- He asks the client deliberate and strategic questions to ensure his understanding of the requirements of each assignment.

- He works on each assignment a little bit and lets it sit for a while.

- His communication with clients conveys composure. You do not hear Jonathan sounding overwhelmed or complaining about his work load.

- He sends a preliminary draft to the client asking for feedback instead of sending a finished product.

Jonathan's first draft deliverables are mostly spot on because of his deliberate and composed approach.

Success Story Discussion Questions

What is one thing that Jonathan does that contributes most to his success?

What is one thing Jonathan does that you like the most?

Introduction

Our daily life is filled with a mixture of activities. Some activities are really important and of high priority. Others are not as important. It is obvious that we should focus our time, energy, and attention on the most important activities.

A person with a perfectionist tendency approaches every activity with a perfectionist approach, which slows down getting anything accomplished to meet established deadlines. Moreover, working with and working for a perfectionist can be very stressful due to unreasonable expectations and demands for everything to be perfect.

The purpose of this chapter is to advocate for the pursuit of excellence as an alternative to a perfectionist approach. Simply defined, the pursuit of excellence is a step by step iterative approach to achieve extraordinary outcomes.

What is perfection vs. excellence?

Perfection is expecting oneself or others to produce a desired outcome during the first attempt. Excellence is iteratively working toward producing a valuable outcome.

What is perfectionism?

In his book titled, *Moving Past Perfect*, Greenspon defines perfectionism as follows: "Perfectionism is not about doing our best. It's not about the struggle for excellence, or the healthy striving for high goals. Perfectionism is about believing that if we can just do something perfectly, other people will love and accept us – and if we can't, we'll never be good enough. Perfectionism is a burden that takes a heavy toll. Personal relationships are strained. Intimacy is elusive. Work seems overwhelming. Creativity slows to a trickle. Physical exhaustion is common. Perfectionism is painful and debilitating – a no-win situation."

According to Monica Frank, perfectionism is the individual's belief that he or she must be perfect to be acceptable. Perfectionism is black and white with no gray area. Anything other than perfect is failure. Perfectionism is an attitude, not necessarily a behavior. In other words, two people can engage in the same behavior, such as trying to win an Olympic gold medal, but one can be pursuing excellence and the other is demanding perfection. The difference lies in the thought process about the goal or behavior, not in the goal or behavior itself.

What is the pursuit of excellence?

Thirty years ago, Tom Peters published an incredibly influential business book, *In Search of Excellence.* In it, he defined eight characteristics of excellent companies: a bias for action, staying close to the customer, autonomy and entrepreneurship, productivity through people, clear and compelling organizational values, focusing on what you do best, operating with a lean staff, and finding a balance between having enough structure without getting stuck in it.

According to Holly Green, in today's world, excellence is more than a set of principles. It's a set of beliefs, ways of thinking, a matter of discipline, and ways of focusing. Excellence starts with getting very clear on the end state you wish to achieve (winning) and relentlessly driving towards it every day. Excellence requires knowing when to push on (even when you don't have all the information or the perfect solution), but doing it well and constantly refining as you forge ahead. Excellence means accepting only the best, and understanding that when it is not given that you, as the leader, are at least partly responsible.

Pursuing excellence may require tremendous effort and focus as well as other resources. But, unlike perfectionism, it does not demand a sacrifice of self-esteem as it tends to focus on the process of achievement rather than the outcome.

A side by side comparison of perfection vs. excellence

Factor	Perfection	Excellence
Desired Outcome	Flawless	Useful
Approach	Strenuous effort	Iterative effort
Impact on People	Stressful	Fun
Purpose	To impress	To improve
Popular Quote	Do it right the first time	Quality is a journey not a destination
Effect	Negative effect	Positive effect
Flexibility	Inflexible	Flexible
Mistakes	Not tolerated	Welcomed
Process/Results	Results-oriented	Process-oriented
Feeling	Doubt	Confidence
Objectivity	Judgmental	Objective
Spontaneity	Control	Spontaneous
Means-Ends	Destination	Journey
Dynamism	Rigid	Dynamic

What does "perfection is the enemy of good" mean?

"Perfection is the enemy of good" seems counterintuitive but refers to the fact that often people freeze when trying to accomplish important tasks due to not having perfect circumstances. Ecclesiastes 11: 4 instructs, "If you wait for perfect conditions, you will not get anything done."

What "perfection is the enemy of good" does not mean

This author understands that some readers of this chapter may not be fans of this adage. Their position may be due to experiencing or perceiving the adage being used as justification for mediocrity, incompetence, lack of planning, or lack of discipline. These feelings and perceptions are understandable

This author chose to use this adage to advocate the pursuit of excellence to achieve more and to engage people who are not wired to be perfectionists. Thus, "Perfection is the enemy of good" is intended to show the value of excellence, competence, planning, and a disciplined approach through the pursuit of excellence as opposed to perfection for perfection's sake.

Empirical impacts of perfectionism vs. excellence

A Comparative Study between Professional Ballet Dancers and Olympic Standard Triathletes (By Jennifer M. Bolt)

The overall aim of this qualitative research endeavor was to examine the fine line that exists between a positive, healthy striving for excellence versus a debilitating, destructive pursuit of perfection comparatively within the fields of dance and sport. To do so, Bolt conducted several interviews with both professional ballet dancers and Olympic standard triathletes in hopes of illuminating the blurred line that exists between excellence and perfection within dance and sport. Bolt felt that by comparing these two domains one could prevent more serious disorders such as performance anxiety, depression, eating disorders, and even suicide.

Participants in this research were confined to seasoned professionals. These individuals, who had reached a professional status, had arrived at some way of coping, either positively or negatively with the inherent stresses of their work. It was these coping mechanisms that Bolt studied.

The participants in both subcultures revealed recurring patterns concerning their views on the difference between a healthy pursuit of excellence and a debilitating quest for perfection.

Many participants indicated that they had struggled with perfectionistic behavior at some point in their lives. Some admitted to having experienced full-blown perfectionism that had even manifested itself in the form of anorexia or depression. The majority, who indicated this, indicated that any of these maladaptive behaviors were most prominent in early adolescence, which often coincided with the time they decided to train professionally. Lastly, all the participants consistently indicated the correlation between the inherent stresses of their profession with the potential to develop debilitating perfectionistic behavior. Many felt, however, that having a 'perfectionist streak' was in part, a necessary component to achieve high levels within their domain.

By making a clear distinction early on in one's pre-professional training between what is excellence and what is perfection, we may eliminate the chance for developing negative ineffective work habits and destructive and injurious thought patterns that can later manifest themselves in serious psychological problems.

Perfectionism linked to burnout at work, school, and sports

According to research published by the Society for Personality and Social Psychology, concerns about perfectionism can sabotage success at work, school, or on the playing field, leading to stress, burnout, and potential health problems.

In the first meta-analysis of the relationship between perfectionism and burnout, researchers analyzed the findings from 43 previous studies conducted over the past 20 years. It turns out that perfectionism isn't all bad. One aspect of perfectionism called "perfectionistic strivings" involves the setting of high personal standards and working toward those goals in a proactive manner. These efforts may help maintain a sense of accomplishment and delay the debilitating effects of burnout, the study found.

The dark side of perfectionism, called "perfectionistic concerns," can be more detrimental when people constantly worry about making mistakes, letting others down, or not measuring up to their own impossibly high standards, said lead researcher Andrew Hill, an associate professor of sport psychology at York St. John University in England. Previous research has shown that perfectionistic concerns and the stress they generate can contribute to serious health problems, including depression, anxiety, eating disorders, fatigue and even early mortality. This study was published online in the *Personality and Social Psychology Review*.

"Perfectionistic concerns capture fears and doubts about personal performance, which creates stress that can lead to burnout when people become cynical and stop caring," Hill said. "It also can interfere with relationships and make it difficult to cope with setbacks because every mistake is viewed as a disaster."

The study found that perfectionistic concerns had the strongest negative effects in contributing to burnout in the workplace, possibly because people have more social support and clearly defined objectives in education and sports. A student can be rewarded for hard work with a high grade, or a tennis player can win the big match, but a stellar performance in the workplace may not be recognized or rewarded, which may contribute to cynicism and burnout.

"People need to learn to challenge the irrational beliefs that underlie perfectionistic concerns by setting realistic goals, accepting failure as a learning opportunity, and forgiving themselves when they fail," Hill said. "Creating environments where creativity, effort, and perseverance are valued also would help."

Dr. Thomas Curran, Lecturer in Sport Psychology at the University of Bath and co-author of the study, added: "As a society we tend to hold perfectionism as a sign of virtue or high achievement. Yet our findings show that perfectionism is a largely destructive trait. We suggest its effects can be managed and organizations must be clear that perfection is not a criteria of success. Instead, diligence, flexibility and perseverance are far better qualities."

Most people display some characteristics of perfectionism in some aspect of their lives, but perfectionistic strivings or concerns may be more dominant. The development of a personality profile that identified perfectionistic concerns might be a valuable tool in detecting and helping individuals who are prone to burnout.

Perfectionism may link to suicide

In one 2007 study, researchers conducted interviews with the friends and family members of people who had recently killed themselves. Without prompting, more than half of the deceased were described as "perfectionists" by their loved ones. Similarly, in a British study of students who committed suicide, 11 out of the 20 students who'd died were described by those who knew them as being afraid of failure.

In another study, published last year, more than 70 percent of 33 boys and young men who had killed themselves were said by their parents to have placed "exceedingly high" demands and expectations on themselves – traits associated with perfectionism.

Learning organizations learn from mistakes

Argyris and Schon have conducted research with the framework of an organization itself doing the learning. In their perspective, an organization is learning when its members are in organizational roles acting on behalf of the organization. They found that in order for learning to continue over time, an organization must create a culture where mistakes are considered opportunities for feedback and growth and its members are not penalized for reflecting critically upon their individual contributions to organizational problems.

Perfectionism and longevity

A Canadian study that was published in the *Journal of Health Psychology* linked the trait of perfectionism to increased likelihood of premature death! This is presumably because of the massively increased stress perfectionism inflicts. So, overcoming perfectionism may help not only your mental health, but also your very physical survival. One of the tyrannies of perfectionism is the way that it narrows focus to all-or-nothing levels – this has serious consequences.

Perfectionism vs. healthy striving

According to the University of Texas at Austin Counseling and Mental Health Center, *perfectionism* has the following characteristics:

- Set standards beyond reach and reason.

- Never being satisfied by anything less than perfection.

- Become depressed when faced with failure or disappointment.

- Be preoccupied with fears of failure and disapproval.

- See mistakes as evidence of unworthiness.

- Become overly defensive when criticized.

According to The University of Texas at Austin Counseling and Mental Health Center, *healthy striving* has the following characteristics:

- Setting standards that are high but within reach.

- Enjoying process as well as outcome.

- Bouncing back quickly from failure or disappointment.

- Keeping normal anxiety and fear of failure within bounds.

- Seeing mistakes as opportunities for growth and learning.

- Reacting positively to helpful criticism.

Multidimensional perfectionism and burnout

According to Maslachi and Jackson, burnout is described as having three core symptoms:

1) emotional exhaustion

2) cynicism

3) low evaluation of personal competence.

Perfectionism is a combination of exceedingly high standards and a preoccupation with extreme self-critical evaluation. Perfectionism has multidimensional traits including:

a) perfectionistic strivings

b) perfectionistic concerns.

Perfectionistic strivings include positive emotional experiences, active coping strategies, and greater performance. Perfectionistic concerns are associated with an array of maladaptive outcomes. These include almost the converse of perfectionistic strivings such as greater appraisals, anxiety, and avoidant coping.

In a meta-analysis of the relationship between perfectionism and burnout, research shows perfectionistic concerns displayed a positive relationship with symptoms of burnout.

Myths and realities about perfectionism

The Vick Center for Strategic Advising & Career Counseling Blog identifies the following myths and realities about perfectionism:

MYTH: I wouldn't be as successful if I weren't such a perfectionist.

REALITY: There is no evidence that perfectionists are more successful than their non-perfectionistic counterparts. In fact, there is evidence that given similar levels of talent, skill and intellect, perfectionists perform less successfully than non-perfectionists.

MYTH: Perfectionists get things done, and they do things right.

REALITY: Perfectionists tend to be "all or nothing" thinkers. They see events and experiences as either good or bad, perfect or imperfect, with nothing in between. Such thinking often leads to procrastination, because demanding perfection of oneself can quickly become overwhelming. A student who struggles with perfectionism may turn in a paper weeks late (or not at all) rather than on time with less than perfect sentences. A perfectionist employee may spend so much time agonizing over some noncritical detail that a project misses its deadline.

MYTH: Perfectionists are determined to overcome all obstacles to success.

REALITY: Perfectionistic behaviors increase one's vulnerability to depression, writer's block, performance and social anxiety, and other barriers to success. These blocks to productivity and success result from the perfectionist's focus on the final product. Instead of concentrating on the process of accomplishing a task, perfectionists focus exclusively on the outcome of their efforts. This relentless pursuit of the ultimate goal can seriously hinder their efforts.

Strategies to fight perfectionism

Increase your awareness of the self-critical nature of your all or nothing thoughts, and how they extend to other people in your life.

- Learn to substitute more realistic, reasonable thoughts for your habitually critical ones.

- When you find yourself criticizing a less than perfect performance (whether your own or someone else's), make yourself stop and think about the good parts of that performance.

- Then ask yourself questions such as: Is it really as bad as I feel it is? How do other people see it? Is it a reasonably good performance for the person(s) and circumstances involved?

Be realistic about what you can do. By setting more realistic goals, you will gradually realize that "imperfect" results do not lead to the punitive consequences you expect and fear.

- Suppose you swim laps every day for relaxation and exercise. You set yourself the goal of 20 laps, even though you can barely swim 15.

- If you are a perfectionist, you soon may feel disappointed at your performance and anxious about improving it.

- Because you're focused on the outcome, you gain little sense of fun or satisfaction from your efforts. You may even give up swimming because you're not "good enough."

- A healthier approach would be to tell yourself that 15 laps is good enough for now. So you continue swimming without anxiety.

- You don't necessarily stop trying to improve, but you swim mainly for exercise and relaxation – for however many laps you can.

Set strict time limits on each of your projects.

- When the time is up, move on to another activity. This technique reduces the procrastination that typically results from perfectionism.

- Suppose you must find references for a term paper and also study for an exam. Set time limits. For example: Decide that you will spend only two hours looking up references, then four (and only four) more hours studying for the test.

- If you stick to your time limits, you won't spend the entire day searching for elusive references, nor try to study late at night when you are too tired to be effective.

Learn how to deal with criticism.

- Perfectionists often view criticism as a personal attack, which leads them to respond defensively.

- Concentrate on being more objective about the criticism and about yourself.

- Remind yourself that if you stop making mistakes, you also stop learning and growing.

- Remember that criticism is a natural thing from which to learn, rather than something to be avoided at all costs.

Forgive yourself in your moments of imperfections.

- You are bound to make mistakes and lots of them in life and every day.

- Make a habit of forgiving your limitations and your imperfections.

Forgive others' imperfections.

- Practice forgiving others around you when they make mistakes.

- If you walk around judging and criticizing others, you become a source of stress for others.

- Remember, forgiving others is easier on others and on yourself

Develop humor.

- You have to laugh at yourself occasionally.

- Everything in life and every mistake is not a big deal.

- See the funny side of things.

- Humor is relaxing and shows your friendly side.

Learn from mistakes.

- Mistakes are a great school.

- Learning from your mistakes allows you to become wiser and more insightful over a long period of time.

How to transform oneself from perfectionism to excellence

1) Mistakes are a good school. Welcome them. Learn from the mistakes you make in the early stages of your activities.

2) Try. Try. Try. Give yourself the license to try things rather than thinking too long before taking action.

3) Seek inputs from others on how you can improve. Seek inputs from diverse sources. It is helpful to hear from your fans as well as your detractors. Your detractors may provide the best inputs.

4) Considering someone's input is huge. Considering is not necessarily agreeing. Weigh all inputs with an open mind.

5) Incorporate inputs into your actions. The more inputs you incorporate into your worthy action, the stronger your solution.

6) Celebrate small achievements. This creates forward momentum for your cause.

7) Give credit to those who help you along the way.

8) Walk away from stressful situations.

9) Create joyful moments.

Concluding Remarks

Perfection is expecting oneself or others to produce a desired outcome during the first attempt; while excellence is iteratively working toward producing a valuable outcome. Some terms that are associated with the concept of perfection are: stressful, to impress, inflexible, intolerant, doubt, judgmental, and control. Some words that are associated with excellence are: useful, improve, iterate, flexible, confidence, and dynamic.

Some of the consequences of perfectionist behavior include: performance anxiety, burn-out, depression, eating disorders, and even suicide.

Coping strategies to turn from perfectionist behavior to the pursuit of excellence include:

- Increase your awareness of the self-critical nature of your all or nothing thoughts, and how they extend to other people in your life.

- Be realistic about what you can do. By setting more realistic goals, you will gradually realize that "imperfect" results do not lead to the punitive consequences you expect and fear.

- Set strict time limits on each of your projects. When the time is up, move on to another activity.

- Learn how to deal with criticism. Perfectionists often view criticism as a personal attack, which leads them to respond defensively.

While perfectionism is likely to jeopardize the wellbeing of individual contributors, teams, and organizations, the pursuit of excellence is likely to benefit all involved.

End of Chapter Activity

1. *Why is excellence better than perfectionism?*

2. *Write 3-5 actions you will take to adopt healthy strivings?*

3. *What would you share with your colleague who may have perfectionist tendencies?*

References

Greenspon, T. Moving Past Perfect. How Perfectionism May Be Holding Back Your Kids (and You!) and What You Can Do About It. Free Spirit Publishing, USA. 2014

Interview with Thomas Greenspon on Perfectionism
http://www.davidsongifted.org/Search-Database/entry/A10790

Ben-Shahar, B. The Pursuit of Perfect: How to Stop Chasing Perfection and Start Living a Richer, Happier Life, 2009, McGraw Hill Publishing, USA

Redefining Excellence for Today's World
http://www.forbes.com/sites/work-in-progress/2012/03/06/redefining-excellence-for-todays-world/#776eb4242d85

Excellence Vs. Perfection by Monica Frank
https://www.excelatlife.com/articles/excellence.htm

Excellence Vs. Perfection by Habits for Wellbeing
http://www.habitsforwellbeing.com/excellence-vs-perfection/

The Alarming New Research on Perfectionism
http://nymag.com/scienceofus/2014/09/alarming-new-research-on-perfectionism.html

Myths and Realities About Perfectionism
https://sites.utexas.edu/ugs-csa/2013/02/01/myths-and-realities-about-perfectionism/

Fry, P. & Debats, D. (2009) Perfectionism and the Five-factor Personality Traits as Predictors of Mortality in Older Adults Journal of Health Psychology May 2009 vol. 14 no. 4

How to Overcome Perfectionism in Everyday Ways
http://www.uncommonhelp.me/articles/overcoming-perfectionism/

How to Overcome Perfectionism: 8 Strategies for Making Better Life
http://www.huffingtonpost.com/tamar-chansky/perfectionism_b_1556414.html

> *If you want to increase your success rate, double your failure rate.*
>
> — Tal Ben-Shahar

Appendix of Self Assessments

From Chapter 1 - Rate Your Current Practice of *Become What You Say*

Rate your current practice of *Become What You Say* actions on a scale of 1 to 5.

(1=Poor, 2=Below Average, 3=Average, 4=Good, 5=Excellent)

Become What You Say Actions	1=Poor 5=Excellent
1. When you encounter challenging situations, you tend to reframe the situation to express yourself in appreciative terms.	1 2 3 4 5
2. You frequently reflect on your successes in life to plan your future pursuits.	1 2 3 4 5
3. You believe that what and when you give makes a difference.	1 2 3 4 5
4. You readily express gratitude to people you meet in person and virtually, including online communications, emails, texts, and phone conversations.	1 2 3 4 5
5. In networking conversations, you make personal connections by trying to learn more about the person than simply what they do.	1 2 3 4 5
6. You are good at finding a common ground with your rivals.	1 2 3 4 5
7. You volunteer in at least one cause that benefits others.	1 2 3 4 5
8. You maintain positive and constructive communication with your frenemies.	1 2 3 4 5
9. You see mistakes as opportunities for growth and learning	1 2 3 4 5
10. You celebrate small achievements	1 2 3 4 5

Your total score is _____

Assess your score:

40 +	Outstanding
30 +	Very Good
25 +	Good
Below 25	Needs Improvement

From Chapter 2 - Rate Your Current Level of Positive Self-Talk

(1=Poor, 2=Below Average, 3=Average, 4=Good, 5=Excellent)

Positive Self Talk Actions	1=Poor 5=Excellent (Circle One)
1. You always think before you speak, even jokingly.	1 2 3 4 5
2. You know the difference between negative self-talk and positive self-talk.	1 2 3 4 5
3. When in doubt about saying something, you make positive statements about yourself and others.	1 2 3 4 5
4. When you encounter challenging situations, you reframe the situation to express yourself in appreciative terms.	1 2 3 4 5
5. You know the roles in which you naturally excel.	1 2 3 4 5
6. You invest more time in the areas where you have the most potential for greatness.	1 2 3 4 5
7. You are quick to get over a setback and try again.	1 2 3 4 5
8. You resist distractions that prevent you from achieving your goals.	1 2 3 4 5
9. You are open to learning from your experiences and from those around you.	1 2 3 4 5
10. You seize the opportunity to do what you do best, every day.	1 2 3 4 5

Your total score is _____

Assess your score:

40 +	Outstanding
30 +	Very Good
25 +	Good
Below 25	Needs Improvement

From Chapter 3 - Rate Your Current Level of Reflective Planning

(1=Poor, 2=Below Average, 3=Average, 4=Good, 5=Excellent)

Reflective Planning Actions	1=Poor 5=Excellent (Circle One)
1. You have personal interest goals.	1 2 3 4 5
2. You have community interest goals.	1 2 3 4 5
3. You know how to write SMART goals.	1 2 3 4 5
4. You frequently reflect on your successes in life to plan your future pursuits.	1 2 3 4 5
5. You frequently reflect on the proudest moments of your life in general.	1 2 3 4 5
6. You frequently reflect on the proudest moments of your career life.	1 2 3 4 5
7. You frequently reflect on your strengths.	1 2 3 4 5
8. You frequently reflect on the strengths of people around you.	1 2 3 4 5
9. You frequently reflect on the positive contributions people around you make to your well-being.	1 2 3 4 5
10. You frequently reflect on the positive contributions of organizations you work with.	1 2 3 4 5

Your total score is _____

Assess your score:

40 +	Outstanding
30 +	Very Good
25 +	Good
Below 25	Needs Improvement

From Chapter 4 - Rate Your Current Level of Generosity

(1=Poor, 2=Below Average, 3=Average, 4=Good, 5=Excellent)

Generosity Actions	1=Poor 5=Excellent (circle one)
1. Your acts of generosity includes taking care of yourself by taking care of your spiritual and emotional needs.	1 2 3 4 5
2. You spend time with people in need.	1 2 3 4 5
3. You give first from what you earn before you start spending it.	1 2 3 4 5
4. You intentionally seek to own less material possessions.	1 2 3 4 5
5. You understand your success is more than your material possessions.	1 2 3 4 5
6. You spend time considering the needs of others.	1 2 3 4 5
7. You are content with your current material possessions.	1 2 3 4 5
8. You readily give emotional lift to the people around you.	1 2 3 4 5
9. You believe what and when you give makes a difference.	1 2 3 4 5
10. You are engaged in a volunteer activity that makes a difference for others.	1 2 3 4 5

Your total score is _____

Assess your score:

40 +	Outstanding
30 +	Very Good
25 +	Good
Below 25	Needs Improvement

From Chapter 5 - Rate Your Current Level of Gratitude

(1=Poor, 2=Below Average, 3=Average, 4=Good, 5=Excellent)

Gratitude Actions	1=Poor 5=Excellent (circle one)
1. You readily thank family members for who they are as well as what they do for you and what they do for others.	1 2 3 4 5
2. You frequently thank your colleagues for their contributions as well as for who they are.	1 2 3 4 5
3. You thank your direct reports, protégés, children, etc., for their accomplishments and for their efforts.	1 2 3 4 5
4. You often thank your friends for their friendship as well as for what they do for you and what they do for others.	1 2 3 4 5
5. You express gratitude for what your organizational leaders accomplish and for their efforts.	1 2 3 4 5
6. You often express gratitude to the customers who buy your services and products.	1 2 3 4 5
7. You readily thank people in places where you buy products and receive services from others.	1 2 3 4 5
8. You readily thank casual acquaintances for their accomplishments and their efforts.	1 2 3 4 5
9. You readily express gratitude to people you communicate with virtually including emails, texts, and phone conversations,	1 2 3 4 5
10. Your prayers contain more praise and worship and less requests and demands for your benefit and for the benefit of your loved ones.	1 2 3 4 5

Your total score is _____

Assess your score:

40 +	Outstanding
30 +	Very Good
25 +	Good
Below 25	Needs Improvement

From Chapter 6 - Rate Your Current Level of Networking

(1=Poor, 2=Below Average, 3=Average, 4=Good, 5=Excellent)

Networking Actions	1=Poor 5=Excellent (circle one)
1. While networking, you unplug from electronic devices.	1 2 3 4 5
2. When attending professional meetings, you choose to sit next to people you do not know.	1 2 3 4 5
3. You point out what you have in common with others.	1 2 3 4 5
4. You engage in strategic bragging when the opportunity presents itself.	1 2 3 4 5
5. When you do not agree, you ask more *why* and *how* questions rather than immediately engaging in debate.	1 2 3 4 5
6. When you meet people, you pay attention to their names and try to remember them.	1 2 3 4 5
7. After a professional meeting, you follow up by delivering what you promised.	1 2 3 4 5
8. During conversations, you are totally focused on the person. No multi-tasking.	1 2 3 4 5
9. When you meet people you express warmth with smiles and friendly gestures.	1 2 3 4 5
10. In networking conversations, you make personal connections by trying to learn more about the person than simply what they do.	1 2 3 4 5

Your total score is _____

Assess your score:

40 +	Outstanding
30 +	Very Good
25 +	Good
Below 25	Needs Improvement

From Chapter 7 - Rate Your Current level of Coopetition-Oriented Teamwork

(1=Poor, 2=Below Average, 3=Average, 4=Good, 5=Excellent)

Coopetition-Oriented Teamwork Actions	1=Poor 5=Excellent (circle one)
1. You successfully work with team members who possess very divergent attributes such as nationality, gender, religion, ethnicity, and professional backgrounds.	1 2 3 4 5
2. You have a positive experience in successfully accomplishing very complex and and very important interests of importance to society.	1 2 3 4 5
3. You are good at finding a common ground with your rivals.	1 2 3 4 5
4. You maintain positive and constructive communication with your frenemies.	1 2 3 4 5
5. You maintain supportive and encouraging interpersonal relationships with all stakeholders.	1 2 3 4 5
6. You empower team members to make decisions and be accountable for their actions.	1 2 3 4 5
7. You are aligned with and believe in the mission of the team.	1 2 3 4 5
8. You encourage team members with complementary skills.	1 2 3 4 5
9. You foster a culture of mutual respect for all stakeholders regardless of a person's role.	1 2 3 4 5
10. You adopt a common approach based on inputs from stakeholders with differing strengths.	1 2 3 4 5

Your total score is _____

Assess your score:

40 +	Outstanding
30 +	Very Good
25 +	Good
Below 25	Needs Improvement

From Chapter 8 - Rate How Well You Give Back to Your Community

On a scale of 1 to 5, rate how well you give back by circling your choices

(1=Poor, 2=Below Average, 3=Average, 4=Good, 5=Excellent)

Your Level of Engagement	1= Poor 5= Excellent (Circle Your Choice)
1. You have discovered your sense of purpose.	1 2 3 4 5
2. Most of your career and personal activities support your sense of purpose.	1 2 3 4 5
3. You volunteer in at least one cause that benefits others.	1 2 3 4 5
4. Your volunteer activities are balanced with the rest of your life.	1 2 3 4 5
5. You are actively engaged in community advocacy.	1 2 3 4 5
6. Your community advocacy activities are balanced with the rest of your life.	1 2 3 4 5
7. You engage in conversations about matters you have some control over.	1 2 3 4 5
8. You engage in conversations where you are either learning from others or sharing insights.	1 2 3 4 5
9. You properly manage a balance between your community and you personal commitments.	1 2 3 4 5
10. You have direct experience with the benefits of giving back to the community.	1 2 3 4 5

Your total score is _____

Assess your score:

40 +	Outstanding
30 +	Very Good
25 +	Good
Below 25	Needs Improvement

From Chapter 8 - Rate Your Current Success as Volunteer

On a scale of 1 to 5, rate how well you serve as a volunteer by circling your choices

(1=Poor, 2=Below Average, 3=Average, 4=Good, 5=Excellent)

Your Level of Success as a Volunteer	1= Poor 5= Excellent (Circle Your Choice)
1. Your reason for volunteering with this organization is clear to you and to the target organization.	1 2 3 4 5
2. You have adequate time to dedicate to this organization.	1 2 3 4 5
3. You constantly prioritize your role and assignments.	1 2 3 4 5
4. You and the target organization have mutually agreed on your role and assignments.	1 2 3 4 5
5. When necessary, you seek clarification about your role and assignments.	1 2 3 4 5
6. When necessary, you seek to renegotiate your role and assignments.	1 2 3 4 5
7. When necessary, you seek clarification of what is expected of you.	1 2 3 4 5
8. After completion of assignments, you seek and obtain feedback about your performance.	1 2 3 4 5
9. You are generally satisfied with your volunteer engagement.	1 2 3 4 5
10. As a result of your volunteer role and assignments, you feel like you are making a positive difference in the lives of people and contributing to society.	1 2 3 4 5

Your total score is _____

Assess your score:

40 +	Outstanding
30 +	Very Good
25 +	Good
Below 25	Needs Improvement

From Chapter 9 - Rate Your Current Level of Excellence Over Perfection

(1=Poor, 2=Below Average, 3=Average, 4=Good, 5=Excellent)

Excellence Over Perfection Actions	1= Poor 5= Excellent (Circle Your Choice)
1. You set standards that are high but within reach.	1 2 3 4 5
2. You enjoy process as well as outcome.	1 2 3 4 5
3. You bounce back quickly from failure or disappointment.	1 2 3 4 5
4. You keep normal anxiety or fear of failure within bounds.	1 2 3 4 5
5. You see mistakes as opportunities for growth and learning.	1 2 3 4 5
6. You create joyful moments in your work.	1 2 3 4 5
7. You celebrate small achievements.	1 2 3 4 5
8. You give credit to those who help you along the way.	1 2 3 4 5
9. You weigh all inputs with an open mind.	1 2 3 4 5
10. You welcome making early stage mistakes.	1 2 3 4 5

Your total score is _____

Assess your score:

40 +	Outstanding
30 +	Very Good
25 +	Good
Below 25	Needs Improvement

Book Testimonials

"It's impossible not to be swept up in the wake of Dr. Hamda's practice of using positive words, actions and attitudes as an approach to building successful business and community relationships! Fortunately, you don't need to have the privilege of working directly with Dr. Hamda to experience how making "positive adjustments" in how you think and communicate can result in productive and satisfying results. As a learning leader, a driving principle that underscores the advice I give to my clients is to always adopt practices that ensure sustainable learning. Become What You Say gives you the field-tested tools and advice you need to achieve sustainable personal and professional growth. With gratitude."

— Natalia Guerrido-CEO and Partner, Bonzach LLC

"Gabe has remained more optimistic than anyone I know, in any situation. NEVER in the 20 years I have worked with him have I heard him bad-mouth a person. Never! Can you imagine! Not everyone we come across in our lives is a positive character, but Gabe sees the best in everyone. His positive attitude is contagious, as it sets the stage for a happy, hopeful organizational culture. Using positive words is a way to shape productive behavior, and he is a wonderful role model for that."

— Tanya E. Kruk, MA, CAPM, Senior Consultant

"If you know Dr. Hamda, his words in this book in it's second edition remind you of the positive words he says whenever he greets you. You can't help but smile as he greets you. This book is a printed memory of when you and he meet. Become What You Say continues the tradition of the first edition with more examples, insights, and research on the power of words, how they influence one's own attitude, and shape the behavior of others. This book is, first and foremost, inspirational -- coupled with instructional and motivational elements to yield a triple outcome for the reader."

— Stuart H. Weinstein, Ph.D., Graduate Faculty, Instructional Systems Development,
University of Maryland Baltimore County

"I've known Gabe Hamda close to a decade. He understands the power of words. Not only does he always maintain a positive tone in his talks, but he also encourages everyone he meets to use positive words. In 'Become What You Say', Gabe will show you how to become what you want by knowing how to say it right."

— Assegid Habtewold, the author of
'The Highest Level of Greatness' and 'Soft Skills That Make or Break Your Success'

"I have known Gabe Hamda for almost twenty years. He has been an inspiration and partner in a number of business ventures. When I took over the leadership of Jacksonville Fire and Rescue Services, after retiring as Fire Chief of the District of Columbia Fire and Emergency Medical Services Department, my initial task was to begin Team Building. I called on Gabe and his team to assist. His untiring energy and willingness to assist was of tremendous help to my success in

building a strong team, that would help make Jacksonville Fire and Rescue Department one on the best in the nation. I find him to be the most optimistic and generous person, and business leader I have known. His willingness to give advice and share his knowledge with new and upcoming businesses is unprecedented. I am eternally grateful for his friendship."

— Ray Alfred, Fire Chief (Ret.), President, Emergency Responders Industries, Inc.

If a more positive person in word or deed than Dr Gabe Hamda exists, I am eagerly awaiting them. I have known him and heard his uplifting speech and wondered, is this real? Well, he is real, the full frontal display of optimism and positive example. The lessons of his book promise success. I will gladly read and heed.

— Gene Kendall, Radm USN(ret)

You Become What You Say: The Power of Words by Dr. Hamda is a special gift because it distills the wisdom of a very exceptional thought leader. Dr. Hamda is a successful businessman and over the years that I have known him, he has generously volunteered his time to mentor and support the development of others. He is a wonderful example of a leader who "walks his talk". In this book, he takes us on a journey unlike any other that will enrich your soul and bring out your true brilliance. Please don't rush your reading, I encourage you to take your time and savor the genius of this book.

- James Alexander, Internal Organization Development Consultant, Federal Government

"I have known Gabe Hamda for over 15 years and find him to be one of the most positive, generous, and creative business people I have ever met. Gabe's effervescent personality enables him to quickly engage people and establish common ground with both friends and foes. He is well-grounded – intellectually, professionally, socially, and spiritually – and integrates his wealth of life experiences into everything and everyone he touches. Dr. Hamda models the attributes about which he writes in his latest work, You Become What You Say. He operates on the principle "freely you have received, freely give" and has demonstrated such liberality with his time, talents, and treasure. As a developing consultant, I consider Gabe to be a personal mentor from whom I can seek and receive sound counsel on a broad array of business and professional topics. I can honestly say that Gabe Hamda doesn't just talk the talk, he walks the walk!"

— Verdun P. Woods, Jr. Organizational Development Consultant, Jacksonville, FL